Discovering the
3EEE Lifestyle

THE MAKING OF A DISCIPLE

JOEL NELSON

ISBN 978-1-64569-057-3 (paperback)
ISBN 978-1-64569-058-0 (digital)

Christian Faith Publishing, Inc.
832 Park Avenue
Meadville, PA 16335
www.christianfaithpublishing.com

Holy Bible, King James Version, KJV Copyright 1967 by Oxford University Press.

Holy Bible, New International Version, NIV Copyright 1973, 1978, 1984, 2011 by Biblica, Inc.,

Holy Bible, New American Standard Version, NASB Copyright 1977 by J.B. McCabe Company.

Printed in the United States of America

And the things that thou hast heard of me among many witnesses, the same commit thou to faithful men, who shall be able to teach others also. (2 Timothy 2:2, KJV)

Dedication

This book is dedicated to my beloved wife and cherished friend, Ethel, who has faithfully supported and encouraged me in this ministry of making disciples.

Contents

Acknowledgments

My primary support team has always been my family—my wife Ethel and my son, Kevin; my niece, Sandra Reed, for her constant encouragement to complete the task of writing this book.

I am grateful for the elders, leaders, and members of New Destiny Baptist Church where I served as pastor for seven years. New Destiny Baptist Church was the place in which many of the ideas in this book were implemented.

I thank and praise my Lord Jesus Christ for the opportunity to serve him. What a privilege and joy!

Introduction

> Ultimately each church will be evaluated by only one thing, its disciples. Your church is only as good as its disciples. It does not matter how good your praise, preaching, programs or property are. If your disciples are passive, needy, consumerist, and not moving in the direction of radical obedience, your church is not good. (Neil Cole)

The Church of Jesus Christ has been called by God to *exalt* (Isaiah 25:1), *equip* (Ephesians 4:11–13), and *evangelize* (Matthew 28:18–20; John 17:18). God has gifted his church to help people to grow and to proclaim his truth. The 3EEE *development process* looks at how this can be carried out to achieve Jesus Christ's command to his church to make disciples.

This begins by adhering to the Great Commission to make disciples by leading people to a life-changing experience in Jesus Christ that results in an ongoing mature and loving relationship with him.

In his article, "What's driving your church," Rick Warren said, "Leading your church into health and growth won't depend on launching a bunch of new programs and ministries. It will depend on designing and working through a process for making fully mature, reproducing disciples so that you can help people move from the local community into your crowd, from the crowd into your congre-

11

gation, from being part of your congregation to being fully committed to being part of the core of your church."

The Lord never told us to make converts or church members. He called us to make disciples. Being a disciple is God's plan for every Christian. There are only three times in all of the New Testament where believers are referred to as Christians: Acts 11:26, Acts 2:28, and 1 Peter 4:16. The word "disciple" or "disciples" is used 569 times in the New Testament and were the names attached to those who truly believed in Jesus Christ. The Lord fully intended for us to make disciples.

To accomplish this task, you must focus on three primary areas: *exalt* the Savior, *equip* the saints, and *evangelize* the sinner. These are practical steps to help us effectively make disciples.

The motivation is simple! It is to value your love for God, each other, and the lost. With that alone, God's church embraces the two great commandments (Matthew 22:37, 39) and the one great commission (Matthew 28:18–20).

A Christian is one who has come to salvation by faith, trusting in the Lord Jesus Christ as his or her Savior. That person has come to the revelation of God through Jesus Christ. You are not a Christian because you have been baptized or you attend church. But you are a Christian because you have placed your faith in the Lord Jesus Christ. Becoming a Christian is not where the process stops, but coming to Christ is where the process actually begins.

Today, many people equate "becoming a disciple" with "being baptized and received into church membership." A *disciple* is something different. A *disciple* is one who is a lifelong student and follower of Jesus Christ—one who will go wherever Jesus goes, do whatever Jesus does, and will say what Jesus says. The difference between being a disciple and just being a Christian is the position and the practice. Being a Christian is my position in Christ; being a disciple is my life's practice for Christ. The Christian received the life of Christ. The disciple gives their life for Christ. The Christian is one who professes faith. The disciple is one who practices faith. The Christian talks about being saved. The disciple lives like they are saved.

You can't be a disciple without being a believer, but you can be a believer and not be a disciple. You can say all the right things, think all the right things, believe all the right things, do all the right things, and still not follow Jesus Christ. In Luke 6:46, Jesus said, "And why do ye call me Lord, Lord, and do not do the things which I say?" Practice does not match profession! If that is true, why do we spend so little time and effort in preparation for discipleship?

Christian discipleship is the process by which a disciple grows in the Lord Jesus Christ and is equipped by the Holy Spirit, who resides in the heart, helping the believer to overcome the pressures and trials of this present life and become more and more Christlike.

Discipleship begins when we accept Jesus Christ as our personal Savior and it continues throughout our Christian life. We cannot decide whether we will be a disciple because discipleship is not one of our options as a Christian. We can only decide what kind of disciple we will be. Our only choice has to do with what kind of disciple we will be—good or bad.

If you've been changed by Jesus Christ, it should lead to a life that's marked by being a disciple who makes disciples. This makes the preparation for discipleship very important. When a person accepts Jesus Christ as their Savior and Lord, then we must place them alongside another believer to help them learn how to have a daily walk with the Lord; to learn how to begin to discover for themselves the riches of God's Word and how to pray; to help them become part of a local body of believers and be nourished in fellowship and encouragement; to help them learn to discern how Satan deceives us with temptations; to help them to learn the importance of daily surrender of the will, surrender of goals, to seek his direction. Also, to give and to realize that part of the mandate of a relationship with Christ is to carry the Gospel to every nation. We must teach them. Not to disciple a new believer is like having a baby and leaving it in a restaurant or a grocery store to learn to feed himself or herself.

Making disciples is serious business. It is laying the foundation in a believer's life so he or she can grow into spiritual maturity. It is also allowing God to equip the disciple to invest into others.

Discipleship is serious business because it requires us to put Jesus first—even ahead of our family, our possessions, and even our individual lives. God's kingdom must be first priority with those who follow Jesus Christ, and everything else must become second. Discipleship is serious business because it is about your heart. It's about your innermost part changing so that you become more like Jesus. It will cost you everything. This means you cannot hold on to your agenda, your dreams, or your life and expect to become a disciple. A disciple gives up everything to follow Jesus Christ, the Master. In our lives, there are things that we want to hold onto, our attitudes and our dreams that we want to accomplish. You can't have both. You either choose to give yourself to Christ and sacrifice everything for him or not.

There are many people who consider themselves to be followers of Christ but are really not, even though they have made a profession of faith, read their Bibles, pray, and even give an offering, but they are not living and thinking like real disciples. Jesus commands us to go and make disciples. The implication is that "Disciples are made, not born." God may call us from birth to be his children, but someone has to train us to be disciples.

A disciple is one who is disciplined, who conforms to the standards and expectations of his teacher. As disciples of Jesus Christ, we are disciplined by his teachings and his example.

How must a *disciple* follow Jesus Christ? Discipleship begins with a willing heart.

Implicit in the whole matter of discipleship is receiving Jesus Christ as Lord and Savior. We must be willing to give ourselves to him in faith and commitment. Our hearts must be willing before we can become the disciples we must be.

When Jesus began to gather the people around him who would become the nucleus of his ministry, they heard him say, "Follow me!" (Mark 1:17). And they followed him. They had willing hearts. They were willing to follow Jesus. The willing heart is where we always began with God. God wants us to be willing.

That is where discipleship begins. And that is where the preparation of discipleship begins. But this submission of the will to the

Lord is not simply a onetime matter. Jesus said that we must take up our cross daily and follow him. The willing heart is always willing to follow Christ, and to learn more about him, and to seek his will.

The word "disciple" is very similar to the word "discipline." The life of discipleship is a life of discipline. This is the point that Jesus was making in Matthew 16:24, when he said, "If any man would come after me, let him deny himself and take up his cross and follow me."

He demanded more of his true followers than to just follow for the "loaves and fishes." He gave us these instructions, "If you want to be my disciple, deny yourself." The principle is that we have to forsake ourselves. What does it mean to forsake or deny self? The Greek word literally means to "disregard one's interest or act entirely unlike you." While most "translations" use the word deny, it really means "ignore self" or "say no to the things you want" or "put aside your own desires and conveniences."

Denying yourself really means to say "I don't know me." This may include denying things in your life or denying your self-worth. It may also mean denying your feeling or denying your happiness. But denying yourself really means to deny lordship over yourself. That means you must say no to the god who is me. It means a decisive no to everything the god "Me" desires.

When you come to Jesus Christ, you're not in the driver's seat of your life anymore. Paul said in 1 Corinthians 6:19–20, "You are not your own, you are bought with a price therefore glorify God in your body." "The Lord is my shepherd" means that he is in the driver's seat. "The Lord is the strength of my life" means that he is not a passenger, but he is in the driver's seat.

A disciple must die daily to follow Jesus. He said to the twelve disciples in Luke 9:23, "Pick up a cross daily and die on it—because that's following me." Anyone that carries a cross is a condemned man. Jesus was saying, nail yourself on the cross, not only in words, but in deeds. All your old self will die. Christians have to die to self daily in order to live for Christ. We must have the life of Christ in our spirit.

Why must do it daily? It is talking about Jesus being first on your mind when you get up each day, seeking to follow him, choose him, and carry the cross with him all the time, rather than just selectively. Carrying the cross daily means a life that is totally dependent on him and letting him have control of you.

Jesus is asking those who are following him to think of their lives as already dead. He is asking his followers to bury their earthly dreams and hopes; to bury their earthly plans and agendas because he will resurrect your dreams, your hopes, your plans, and your agenda, and he will replace them with new ones.

Jesus continues his call by saying, "Follow *me*." But it is not so simple, nor is it easy, because the disciple must be determined to follow. If you are going to follow Jesus Christ, you are going to have to leave some things behind. Peter and Andrew left their fishing nets; James and John left their father; Matthew left his job as a tax collector; and Paul left his position as a Pharisee.

All of these are examples of things that would have hindered them in their relationship with Jesus, that's why they had to leave it. If you are ever going to have the type of relationship you need with the Lord Jesus Christ, then there are some things you must say goodbye to too.

As his disciple, you must purpose in your heart to follow Jesus Christ. Following him must become your one true objective in life. This is the one thing that determines all that you do.

Discipleship means forsaking everything to follow Jesus Christ. Therefore, disciples are called "Followers" of Christ. Anyone following Jesus Christ is called into a relationship, to be like him. We follow Christ by spending time with him, which results in knowing God and knowing how to live.

Jesus Christ requires his disciples to call other people to follow him. The Apostle Paul said in 2 Timothy 2:2, "And the things that thou hast heard from me among many witnesses, the same commit thou to faithful men, who shall be able to teach others also." Teach what you have been taught, which also means they are to teach them to teach others too.

Jesus ends his saying in Luke 9:24 by saying, "For whosoever will save his life shall lose it; but whosoever will lose his life for my sake, the same shall save it." The question most people ask is, "How do we lose our lives for his sake?" By investing everything we have and everything we are in him and in his Gospel and in his kingdom. This means giving him your car, your home, your bank account; your mouth, your heart, your hands, and your feet. As it has been said and sung, "If you can use anything, Lord you can use me." Paul said in Philippian 3:7, "But what things were gain to me, those I counted loss for Christ."

Developing the 3EEE lifestyle begins with "Exalting the Savior through worship." Worship says it's not about me. It's not about my wants or desires. It's not about my ambitions or plans. It's about me giving everything up for God. Worship is submission. Submission to Christ is the foundation of our relationship with him and the core of true worship. Submitting means that we present ourselves to God for his purposes (Romans 12:1).

Developing the 3EEE lifestyle continues with "Equipping the Saints through the Word." The task of equipping is essentially that of getting people ready to live the Christian life and to do ministry in the world. The operative phrase is found in Ephesians 4:12, to "Equip the saints for the work of ministry." The result of being "equipped" is Christlikeness.

The final step in developing the 3EEE lifestyle is "Evangelizing the Sinner through Witnessing." It has been noted that most Christians never share their faith with nonbelievers or have never led anyone to faith in Jesus Christ. A disciple is taught that it is his or her duty to witness for Jesus Christ. In John 20:21, Jesus spoke to his disciples saying, "As my Father hath sent me, even so send I you." Every disciple is commanded to make disciples by witnessing, mark them by baptism, and mature them by teaching them all the things that Jesus Christ commanded us (Matthew 28:19–20).

Witnessing was so very important to Jesus that he compared his disciples to being fishermen. He said, "Follow me, and I will make you fishers of men" (Matthew 4:19). He also compared his disciples to laborers. He said, "The harvest truly is plenteous, but the laborers are few, pray ye therefore the Lord of the harvest, that he will send forth laborers into His harvest" (Matthew 9:37).

Developing the 3EEE *discipleship lifestyle* requires a transformation of life. It is a process that begins when the believer "deny self, take up the cross daily and follow Christ" as Jesus commanded in Luke 9:23. This means more than just casual attendance at worship or Bible study. But it calls for establishing a daily relationship with Jesus through Bible study, prayer, and practicing spiritual disciplines.

PART 1

Exalting the Savior

And what is the exceeding greatness of his power to us-ward who believe, according to the working of his mighty power,

Which he wrought in Christ, when he raised him from the dead, and set him at his own right hand in the heavenly places,

Far above all principality, and power, and might, and dominion, and every name that is named, not only in this world, but also in that which is to come:

And hath put all things under his feet, and gave him to be the head over all things to the church. (Ephesians 1:19–22, KJV)

Exalting the Savior through Worship

The church exists to exalt Jesus. The word "exalt" means to be raised in rank, character, or status; to elevate to the highest heights. It is to honor God with the fullness of our worship, nothing held back. The purpose of man's existence is to glorify God and to enjoy him forever, or simply put, to worship God!

James MacDonald stated in his book, *Gripped by the Greatness of God*, "The main reason the church has lost it moral vision is because it has lost its high and exalted view of God."

In Philippians 2:9–11, the name of Jesus is to be exalted. God gave Jesus Christ the highest name. Philippians 2:10–11 reveals to us this name. It is a name that will cause all knees to bow and all tongues to confess that Jesus Christ is LORD! In the Greek language, the word lord has a special significance. The caesar(s) or emperors of the Roman Empire were all referred to as Lord Caesar. Not just because they had lots of political power, but because they believed they were all divine. The word Lord also speaks about the sovereignty and power of God. When Paul uses this Greek word, Lord, he was ascribing full deity to Jesus Christ. The world slandered the name Jesus, but God the Father made their slander useless by bestowing his own name upon Jesus.

The name "Jesus" means "God is our salvation!" In the Greek language, he is *the* Christ; in the Hebrew language, he is *the* Messiah. Both are identifying him as the "Anointed One"—our King. He is

Immanuel or "God with us." God has promised to never leave us nor forsake us.

In his resurrection, Jesus Christ was exalted over sin, death, and the grave. In his ascension, Jesus Christ was exalted over time and space. But in his coronation, Jesus Christ was exalted over every name that is named. When someone accepts Jesus Christ as Lord and Savior, part of the process of becoming a disciple is learning what worship is and practicing what worship is. Worship is much too important to hope that new believers will learn what to do, or for us to just tell people that they need to do it. We should teach them how to worship and model worship for them. We need to train new disciples in our churches, not just the content of what biblical worship is, but also how to apply it to their personal lives, both in individual worship and in corporate worship.

You cannot truly worship and be quiet or still. To exalt the Lord requires your personal investment. It involves all of you. Peter expresses the physical and dynamic declaration of God's worth when he says, "But you are a chosen generation, a royal priesthood, a holy nation, a peculiar people; that you should show forth the praises of him who has called you out of darkness into his marvelous light" (1 Peter 2:9). We are to *show forth* his praises, not just say praises. The word "show forth" is one word in Greek, *exaggello*, which literally is "to message forth," or to make known by praising, proclaiming, or celebration. *Aggelos* is angel or "messenger of God" who heralds God's glory. The Hebrew *shofar*, or trumpet, introduced worship with a loud, long blast, so too, we are to trumpet God's praises loudly, just as angels do before the throne. In Psalm 66 verses 1–3, David said, "Make a joyful noise unto God, all ye lands: Sing forth the honor of his name: make his praise glorious. Say unto God, How terrible art thou in thy works! Through the greatness of thy power shall thine enemies submit themselves unto thee." David continues his instruction, "Sing to God, sing praise to his name, extol him who rides on the clouds, rejoice before him" (Psalm 68:4).

Why does God want us to praise him? Because he deserves our praise, and it takes our focus off of self and places it on him. We live in a "selfie" focused world, and we need a consistent reminder that life is not all about us. God desires our eyes be set firmly on him because he is worthy of our praise, no matter what we face from day to day. Praise will affect you; it affects the devil, and it affects God. It touches everything and every part of our lives.

Praise also causes us to be humble. As we praise God as Creator and King, we admit and recognize that we're not in control, but he is. He is above all.

Our faith is not complete without praise. Colossians 2:7 says, "Rooted and built up in him, and established in the faith, as ye have been taught, abounding therein with thanksgiving."

A disciple's first responsibility to God is to worship him. If we haven't learned to be worshipers, it doesn't really matter how well we do anything else. The chief end of man is to glorify God and to enjoy him forever; that is, to worship God! In Revelation 4:11 we read, "Thou art worthy, O Lord, to receive glory and honor and power: for thou hast created all things, and for thy pleasure they are and were created."

In Matthew 4:10, Jesus speaking to Satan said, "Thou shalt worship the Lord thy God, and him only shalt thou serve." God commands that we worship him. He doesn't request it, but instead, he requires it!

Isaiah 52:13 says, "Behold, My Servant will wisely prosper. He will be high and lifted up, and greatly exalted." The word "servant" used here is the Messiah—our Lord Jesus Christ. He is the only one worthy of such high exaltation because of his willing humiliation and sacrifice described in Isaiah 53. He was lifted up in humiliation on the *cross* for man, and God the Father lifted him above all principalities and rule. There is no one more exalted than Jesus Christ. Nor will there ever be throughout all eternity.

Only believers can truly worship God. The direction of worship is from believers to God. We magnify God's name in worship by expressing our love and commitment to him.

Therefore, the process of making disciples should start by teaching the believers to realize the need, privilege, and means of worshiping God in their daily lives.

But what does God value in our worship? God finds true value in our worship when we exalt Jesus Christ as Lord and Savior. All of our worship is through Jesus Christ. We cannot focus our worship on God the Father if it is not through God the Son. In Jesus Christ, God the Father sees us as sanctified, justified, redeemed, and regenerated, and as a result, he accepts our worship.

Philippians 2:9–11 says, "Wherefore God also hath highly exalted him, and given him a name which is above every name, that at the name of Jesus every knee should bow, of things in heaven, and things in earth, and things under the earth and that every tongue should confess that Jesus Christ is Lord, to the glory of God, the Father." Not only will there be a bowing of knees before Jesus, but the name of Jesus will also be confessed by the lips of every creature. Men, angels, and demons alike will join their voices and will, together, exalt the name of Jesus. Jesus is worthy of our worship and praise because he is God and because of what he has done—because he shed his blood to pay the price for our sins and, thereby, offer us eternal life. When we publicly exalt the name of Jesus, we are just getting in on God's plan for Jesus and for his people.

The name Jesus can only be attached to praise, honor, and worship. The church exists to exalt Jesus Christ by honoring him and worshipping him and praising him. The Bible tells us that when the name Jesus is heard, it is to be reverenced through praise and worship. Our desire, our goal is to please him, to exalt him. The Bible tells us that when this name is heard, it is to be reverenced through praise and worship. David said, "O magnify the Lord with me, and let us exalt his name together" (Psalm 34:3). "Exalt the Lord our God, and worship at his footstool; for he is holy" (Psalm 99:5).

In Romans 16:25–27, the Apostle Paul ends the book with an eloquent conclusion, a beautiful doxology, praising God for what he has done through his Son, Jesus Christ. It is a grand finale befitting the Lord God, his Son, the Lord Jesus Christ, and the Gospel by which we come to know them. It proclaims the majestic truth that God purposed from all eternity to save the nations by Jesus Christ.

The word doxology comes from the Greek word *doxa*. It originally meant "an opinion." Your opinion of someone was your doxology regarding that person. Eventually, *doxa* came to refer to a person's reputation or power. Finally, it came to mean honor or glory bestowed on someone.

In the Bible, the *one* who is deserving of *doxa*, or of all honor, glory and power is none other than God. In fact, the word *doxa* appears in the New Testament as something related to or regarding Jesus Christ. It is the response of coming into contact with the Lord God.

Defining Worship

Exalting equals worship! The word worship today comes from the old English word "worth-ship," wherein we engage our mind, emotions, and our will to gratefully acknowledge the worth of our God. No other human activity is as lofty as that of adoring God.

Worship is knowing and loving God back. Today, worship is misunderstood. When you say the word worship, most people think of singing, prayer, ritual or communion, going to church, or something you do in church. But worship is more than all those things.

Worship is a concept that is difficult to define. Do we really know and understand true worship? Apart from the clichés and church slangs, can we really explain to someone what Christian worship is? It has been said that it is better to experience worship than to define it.

Worship, in the broadest sense, is a "meeting between God and God's people." In this meeting, God becomes present, and in response, those who are gathered offer praise and thanksgiving. Thus, the worshipper is brought into personal contact with the *one* who gives meaning and purpose to life. From this encounter, the worshipper receives strength and courage to live with hope in this world.

For anyone to worship the true and living God, it must be based upon a personal relationship with him, or it is meaningless. Worship is a two-way communication between the believer and God. It is a dialogue of response involving both actions and speech. God's presence is revealed and our need for intimacy with him is met and we respond with thanksgiving and praise. God speaks through his Word;

we are convicted, and we repent. God extends mercy through Jesus Christ; we respond with adoration. Real worship provides an opportunity for God and God's people to express their love for each other. In worship, we carry an exchange of love with God who is present, who speaks to us in the here and now, and has done—and continues to do—marvelous things.

In his book, *Real Worship*, Warren Wiersbe defines worship as, "the believers' response of all that they are—mind, emotions, will, and body—to all that God is and says and does."

God is the object of our worship. In Psalm 96:1–9, the writer uses the word Lord throughout these verses. He is directing our attention to the object of our worship. The word Lord in this text is the name *Yahweh*. It's the word Jehovah in the English language. This word *Yahweh* means "to be," as in, "to live." It implies that God is life, and that life is found in him alone. He is the self-existent *one*, He does not need food, air, or water to help him exist. He does not need shelter or clothing to exist. Yahweh! The Jews considered the name so holy that they wouldn't pronounce it for fear they would profane the holiness of God.

Worship to *Yahweh* or Jehovah must include activity that focuses on the praise to God that affirms the worth of God. It is not getting something out of God or bribing him with flattery or looking for a "spiritual fix" to liven an otherwise dull day; but it is our hearts and our mouths and our souls and our bodies telling God directly that he is a great God and he is a good God and he is worthy to receive honor; he is worthy to receive glory; he is worthy to receive praise.

Worship is a verb throughout Scripture. As a verb, it helps us to think of worship as action rather than a passive emotion. It can be expressed both verbally and physically. Angels and cherubim do it constantly before the throne of God. In the book of Revelation, you will find physical and verbal declarations of the worth and holiness of God. People fell down and worshiped the Lord.

The word "worship" translated in the Greek language is the word *proskuneo*. It literally means to kiss toward. It is used in the ancient tradition wherein a person would bow to the ground, bow the head, and kiss the hand of one who was superior to him, such as a king, queen, etc. It was also used in a sense of bowing down or prostrating oneself with honor, respect, awe, reverence, and homage. Simply put, we are to come humbly, daily, no matter where we are, and give homage to God because we recognize his superior standing.

In Psalm 95:6, it shows the worshippers falling down on their faces before God. When you really begin to worship God, you will discover he is not just God our Creator but He is also God our Redeemer and God our Savior. We are the sheep of his pasture. God is our shepherd who pays close attention to each of us personally. This should cause us to bow down in worship and to kneel before the Lord our Maker. Bowing and kneeling helps us get "low" before God, which is really the essence of worship. We accept our place before him while we acknowledge his place before us.

Lots of people go to church thinking they are going to the place of worship, but they do not understand worship. Worship is not dependent upon a place or the presence of certain people, but is determined by the presence of God. The presence of God is not determined by the building, the carpet, the stained glass windows, the cross, the pulpit, the musical instruments, or the pastor. Tony Evans said, "If you limit worship to where you are, the minute you leave that place of worship you will leave your attitude of worship behind like a crumpled-up church bulletin."

Worship is really the "living water" returning to its source. In Ecclesiastes 1:7, Solomon wrote these words, "All the rivers run into the sea; yet the sea is not full; unto the place from whence the rivers come, thither they return again." It's like the hydrological cycle. The water comes down from the clouds in the form of rain or snow or ice. This water fills the river, and it flow down to the seas. The water is evaporated by the sun and goes back into the clouds. Then it falls back to the earth.

It's the same way with our worship. The Spirit of God on the inside of the believers was sent down from Heaven into their hearts. The Spirit moves in us and fills us with the glory of our God. When he does, praise and worship begin to flow out of our hearts, and it goes back up to God the Father. It goes back to the source. It's a cycle—our worship begins with God; it flows to us and in us and through us; and go back up to the Father.

Worship can also be defined as the overflow of a grateful heart. It is the outpouring of a heart that is filled with a sense of God's goodness, greatness, and glory. Psalm 45:1 says, "My heart is indicting a good matter." The King James Bible version used the word indicting. The word "indicting" means "to overflow or to keep moving." It was used to speak of a pot of boiling water. It gives us the idea of our love "boiling over or bubbling up" and ascending to God in the form of praise and worship.

Worship is not really about what we do—something that we can just turn on or off depending on the music or our mental state—but worship is a response to God. It is a response to the presence of God that comes from the heart as you know who God is. Worship is not something that we give to God as if we have something to give.

The Disciple Must Trust in God

In the Scriptures, trust and faith are the same. Your faith in God also reveals your ability to trust him. Proverbs 3:5 says, "Trust in the LORD with all your heart and lean not on your own understanding." When you love someone, you will trust them. If you love God, then you will trust God. "Love thy God with all thy heart and with all thy soul and with all thy mind and with all thy strength," Jesus said in Matthew 22:37. This is the first and the greatest of all the commandments! We are created to love God. We desperately need to love God, and the struggle for some of us is that our love for God has faded.

The word trust in the Hebrew language means "to lean on something with the full body," "to lay upon," or "to rest the full weight upon." In our thinking, the word trust means to rely upon or to have confidence in. But the Hebrew word is stronger. It is the idea of stretching yourself out upon a bed or laying on a hard surface. The word means to put your full weight prostrate on something. To trust in the Lord is to lay everything upon him. Watch this: lay you and your troubles upon him, you and your worries upon him; you and your fears upon him; you and your doubts upon him.

Notice that this calling is for total trust and for total commitment: "Trust in the Lord with all your heart." This tells us: know that God does not want a part-time lover. It's all God—not God and your spouse; God and your children. It's all God. It's not God and your friend; God and your partner. He wants to be your first *love*!

If you are having problems trusting the Lord, then it is because you don't love him; you don't know him. Knowing God can only come from having an intimate relationship with him. There is a distinct difference between knowing God and knowing about God. The more you know someone, the more you will love and trust them.

"And lean not unto thine own understanding" (Proverbs 3:6). We are not to lean, in any way, upon our own wisdom and ability. Such a trust and confidence in ourselves is actually pride. We should not have any manner of confidence in self.

The words "acknowledge him" in Hebrew is a command. It is saying, "In all your ways know him." The word means to know him deeply and intimately. It's the kind of knowing that comes with personal experience. It means to know something through and through.

To acknowledge him also means full disclosure that you know him. Declare him! Declare him in your home, to your family. Declare him to your friends, to your neighbors; to your coworkers on your job, and even in your church.

Acknowledging the Lord means to acknowledge his lordship. In every step that we take in our daily walk, our Lord is not simply with us to help us along the way; but he is also with us to direct us in the way. He is the Lord our God, and we must acknowledge the lordship authority of his will and his direction in all our ways. In all our ways we must yield ourselves as a living sacrifice, and as a faithful servant to him (Romans 12:1).

A Disciple Is a Worshipper

Our highest priority as Christians is to give glory to God, to exalt him by giving him worship.

Worship is our highest calling and has the power to draw us into a deeper understanding of discipleship. If a disciple has not learned to be a worshiper, it doesn't really matter how well he or she does anything else. Every believer should be equipped to practice the spiritual disciplines (prayer, praise, preaching, singing, meditation, etc.) in worship. By engaging in worship, believers are thrust into an environment of becoming intimate with God. God wants us to enjoy him and to have a further revelation of him. He wants "eye contact" with us, our full attention focused face-to-face with him. It is a *holy romance*.

Worship is not optional because it is a constant renewal of our relationship with God by means of communing with him through worship. The chief end of man is to glorify God and to enjoy him forever; that is, to worship God! In Revelation 4:11 we read, "Thou art worthy, O Lord, to receive glory and honor and power: for thou hast created all things, and for thy pleasure they are and were created."

We are to glorify God by responding to the Lord Jesus Christ through exalting him as our Creator, our Savior, and our Lord.

Worship is for God and God alone (see John 4:23). The question should not be, "What do I get out of worship?" but rather, "What can I give to God." When we try to worship God with an attitude that is all about us, we find ourselves coming to the service focused on the music, or the instruments, or on who is doing the preaching. We come like Olympic judges ready to rate the event.

How does the bible say we may worship?

- We lift up our hands in worship (1 Tim. 2:8, Psalm 134:2, Psalm 63:3–5)
- We clap our hands in worship (Psalm 47:1)
- We sing songs and shout in worship (Luke 19:37–40; Psalm 95:1–2)
- We bow down before the Lord in worship (Psalm 95:6–9)
- We be still and be quiet in worship (Psalm 46:10)
- Like David, we dance before God in worship (Psalm 149:3–5)
- We sing new songs before the Lord in worship(Psalm 33:2–4)

The Disciple's Prayer Life

Prayer is a form of worshiping God. True prayer is the essence of worship. While some think of prayer as a way to get what they want, our prayers can be a message to him that we love him and are thankful for everything he has done for us.

Prayer is the breath of discipleship. It is as essential to our spiritual life as breathing is to our physical life. A disciple is a person who accepts Jesus Christ as Lord and Savior but also recognizes him as *high priest* and approaches God the Father in prayer through Jesus Christ.

For the disciple of Jesus Christ, prayer is not an option. In Matthew 6:5–8, three times, Jesus uses the words, "And when you pray." He said, "When you pray," not if you pray or if you feel like praying. Jesus expects his disciples to pray. When Jesus asked his disciples to say, "Hallowed be thy name," he was reminding them of the need to come to the Father in an attitude of worship. He knew that the secret to having a successful day was spending time alone with God the Father (Mark 1:35).

The first purpose of prayer is to honor God's name. Matthew 6:9 says, "Our Father." This is the primary purpose of prayer—to bring *worship* to the name of God. "Hallowed" means "holy"—"May your name be held holy." In other words, "Father, may you be revered and respected because of who you are." A person's *name* is equivalent to their character and their reputation. Therefore, prayer should have the reputation of God's name as its highest goal.

The second purpose of prayer is to help us to realize our dependence on God. We are powerless without prayer, but by praying, we admit our dependence on God. When we pray, we are saying to God the Father, "I need you! I can't handle this situation without you." Jesus prayed because he was dependent on the Father, and therefore, he prayed (John 15:5).

The third purpose of prayer is to develop an intimate relationship with God. God wants an intimate relationship with each one of us. And, in order to have intimacy in a relationship with him, prayer for the disciple is essential. Like a father, God really cares about being with his children.

The fourth purpose of prayer is to make our requests known (Jeremiah 33:3). The Bible says in Philippians 4:6, "Make your requests known to God." And it says in John 16:24, "Ask and you will receive." Have you heard this statement, "Too busy not to pray?" And James 4:2, "You do not have because you do not ask." God wants us to ask. God wants us to rely on him and to come to him knowing that he wants to help us (Hebrews 4:16).

It is true that it can also be a way to ask God about things or for things. Jesus promised in John 14:13, "And whatever you ask in my name, that I will do, that the Father may be glorified in the Son. If you ask anything in my name, I will do it."

Of course, prayer extends beyond just asking God for things. It is a conversation between yourself and God, in such a way that your relationship with him will grow. Prayer is loving God and letting ourselves be loved by him. We must learn that prayer is a love relationship. Just as no friendship can truly grow without fellowship, so is it with our relationship with the Lord.

Prayer is a come-as-you-are affair.

A helpful structure for personal prayer by a disciple can be found in the acrostic ACTS. We can gain a deeper understanding of God through these areas of prayer: *adoration, confession, thanksgiving,* and *supplication.*

Adoration is the place where prayer must start because it recognizes God for who he is. When we adore God, we are appreciating

God for who he is. The prayers of adoration are prayers of praise for who God is, offering to him our highest.

In adoration, our focus is on God—who he is and our worship of him. Adoration takes the focus off of oneself and allows us to behold the beauty of the Lord. We appreciate his majesty and his holiness, and we become aware of our sins. Adoration is following Jesus's instruction in Matthew 6:9 when he said, "Hallowed be thy Name." It seems that adoring God's name should be above all other things in our prayer. Jesus's first concern was God getting the glory he is due. When we take time to praise and worship God in our prayers, we place him where he rightfully belongs.

Included in our prayer is the confession of sins. Confession is the admission that we have trespassed God's law, and we stand in need of forgiveness. The closer we draw to God, the more we will sense our own sinfulness. When the prophet Isaiah came into God's presence, he cried out, "Woe is me, for I am undone!" (Isaiah 6:5). The confession of our sin removes the barriers that would cause God not to hear our prayers. As 1 John 1:9 says, "If we confess our sins, he is faithful and just to forgive us." This is, once again, modeled in the Lord's Prayer. After "Our Father who art in heaven," we find, "Forgive us our sins" (Matthew 6:12).

We may never enter into a conversation with God while we are in a state of sin. Psalm 66:18 tells us, "If I regard iniquity in my heart, the Lord will not hear me." We are commanded to come boldly, but we must come contritely as well. The prayer of confession should be a regular part of our spiritual lives as we are being transformed into the people that God wants us be

Thanksgiving is another step in our prayer to God. One way of showing our thanksgiving to God is through prayer. In thanksgiving, our focus is on what God has done—for us, for others. If we have just confessed our sins to our Father and received his forgiveness, then thanksgiving will be a very natural thing to do. The prayer of thanksgiving helps us to live out of a deep sense of gratitude for all that God has done for us.

Giving thanks means we recognize that we are totally dependent on God, and that everything that goes on in our lives is the product of God's sovereign control, his infinite wisdom, his purposes, and his grace. When we give thanks or show our gratitude for what we have, we prevent our focus from shifting to what we do not have.

The fourth step in prayer is supplication. Supplication is asking God to do something, either for yourself or on behalf of somebody else. It is persevering in prayer, to ask, and to keep on asking. In Philippians 4:6, the Apostle Paul encourages believers to offer prayers of supplication to God, he said, "Be careful for nothing; but in everything by prayer and supplication with thanksgiving let your requests be made known unto God."

Without prayer, we cannot get closer to him. When we began to see prayer as a relationship, then we can understand the exhortation in 1 Thessalonians 5:17, "Pray without ceasing."

In our prayer, we reverence God, and that is what worship is all about. By taking our petitions and thanksgiving to God, we are freely admitting and acknowledging that we are dependent upon, and we trust in him.

In 1 Thessalonians 5:16–18, we are called to pray continually, or in other words, to always be talking with God. God is always there with you and is willing to talk with you at all times. Therefore, prayer should be a part of the disciple's daily life as we express our praise, our needs, and our gratitude to God.

In Matthew 11:28, Jesus said, "Come unto me, all ye that labor and are heavy laden, and I will give you rest. Take my yoke upon you, and learn of me; for I am meek and lowly in heart: and ye shall find rest unto your souls. For my yoke is easy, and my burden is light." A new Christian needs to get to know him better. A believer needs to understand the significance of Christ's person, nature, and ministry. The disciple also needs to understand God's will for us as disciples: learning, following, serving one another, and sharing our faith with others. Nothing glorifies the Lord like the people who trust in him enough to call on him in faith.

Prayer is not easy. It does not come naturally. It must be learned in the school of personal discipline. We must pursue it. We must want it badly enough to sacrifice many of our daily activities to have it.

The prayer life of many believers is sporadic and not very exciting. They are "lukewarm"—at least, when it comes to prayer. Many are yearning and crying out to the Lord, "Lord, teach me to pray." They know about prayer, but don't pray as they ought.

As disciples of Jesus Christ, we should want to learn how to pray and receive God's answer.

Both Jesus and John the Baptist taught their disciples how to pray; we must do the same.

We need to teach others how to pray and get results. Most Christians are not taught how to pray; they only copy patterns of prayers that we have heard others pray. But we need to learn how to be effective in our prayer life. James 5:13–16 says, "Is any among you afflicted? let him pray. Is any merry? Let him sing psalms. Is any sick among you? Let him call for the elders of the church; and let them pray over him, anointing him with oil in the name of the Lord: And the prayer of faith shall save the sick, and the Lord shall raise him up; and if he have committed sins, they shall be forgiven him. Confess your faults one to another, and pray one for another, that ye may be healed. The effectual fervent prayer of a righteous man availeth much."

There are two spiritual exercises in these verses of prayer and praise. Prayer and praise are special privileges for the believer, and there should not be a time in our life when we shouldn't be doing one or the other. In the times of cheerfulness or happiness, let us "sing praises," and in the times of sickness and sufferings, let us "pray."

In Luke 11:1, the disciples of Jesus asked him, "Lord teach us to pray." As he taught the disciples to pray, Jesus started with worship in prayer. Before bringing forth petitions to the Father, Jesus honored him with praise. He said, "Our Father which art in heaven, Hallowed be thy name. Thy kingdom come. Thy will be done, as in heaven, so in earth."

When we worship God in prayer, we take our eyes off of ourselves and our needs and even off of the answer we are seeking from him. Instead, we concentrate on him, his love for us, his power, and his character. Proverbs 15:8 says, "The sacrifice of the wicked is an abomination to the LORD: but the prayer of the upright is his delight." He delights in our prayers.

Believers today ought to pray and ask to be taught how to pray. Dwight L. Moody believed he spoke the feelings of thousands of Christians when he said, they hadn't known what it was to pray. "Teach us" should be the prayer of every Christian heart. If the first disciples of Jesus needed to be taught how to pray, how much more do Christians today need to be taught. When we pray, we strengthen our fellowship and our relationship with the Lord.

Prayer is at the heart of *worship*. Prayer may be spoken, sung, offered in silence, and even acted out. In prayer, we respond to God in many ways.

Knowing the God We Worship

It is possible to know the one that is worthy of praise and worship but never come to know him personally. Knowing God's greatness enables us to properly honor him. Understanding God's holiness helps us to be like him. Embracing God's salvation brings humility and joy to our worship. God wants us to know him. He doesn't want worship that is based on our own imagination. He does not want worship that is based on our opinions and our feelings. He wants worship that is based on the truth of who he is.

John 17:3 says, "Now this is eternal life: that they may know you, the only true God, and Jesus Christ, whom you have sent." Eternal life is knowing God the Father and Jesus Christ, his Son; it is being in relationship with God now and forever. This is not knowing about God but knowing him in a personal way. Eternal life is something we are meant to participate in now and forever. The only thing which changes is our address; we go from earth to heaven when we die.

Ephesians 1:3 says, "Blessed be the God and Father of our Lord Jesus Christ, who hath blessed us with all spiritual blessings in heavenly places in Christ." God plans for us to worship the right God. Notice that Paul says, "The Father of our Lord Jesus Christ."

Thinking correctly about God is important because any false ideas about God is idolatry. In Psalm 50:21, God reproves the wicked man with this accusation: "You thought I was altogether like you." A good summary definition of God is "the Supreme Being; the Creator and Ruler of all that is; the Self-existent one who is perfect in power, goodness, and wisdom."

More than anything else, God wants us to know him in a relationship that is intimate. It is very difficult to love someone if we don't know him or her personally. In knowing the God we worship, the question then becomes for us: who is God?

Psalm 96:5–6 says, "For all the gods of the nations are idols, but the LORD made the heavens. Splendor and majesty are before him; strength and glory are in his sanctuary." In other words, our worship must be toward the one who is worthy, simply because of his identity as the Omnipotent, Omniscient, and Omnipresent One, and not just because God is wealthy and able to meet our needs and answer our prayers. We must focus our worship on the worth of God and not on the wealth of God.

God is to be worshipped because he is the creator of all things, and therefore, he is worthy of the worship of all creation. The belief from the Bible in Genesis 1:1 is that the universe was created by the infinite God, simply by speaking it into existence. This foundational belief as Christians causes us to worship God the Creator instead of his creation. God wants, desires, and seeks the worship of his *creation*. It is *holy* worship and an authentic worship that he is looking for. We were created to worship him and glorify him, and according to Revelation 4:11, we respond in awe, reverence, and honor. God is the center of our lives, the sustainer of our lives.

In Acts 17:28, Paul says, "In him we live and move and have our being." We worship God because he is our creator and sustainer in life.

We worship Jesus Christ because he is the ruler of all creation—"the firstborn of all creation."

Some people have taken this phrase to mean that Jesus was God's first creation—that God created Jesus before he created anything else. That would make Jesus a created being that had a beginning rather than the self-existent eternal God. But by referring to Jesus with the title "firstborn," Paul is saying that Jesus is the ruler of all creation.

One of the important implications of the fourth commandment (Exodus 20:8–11) is God determined that a day be set apart to worship him because he worked as creator for six days, and then rested on the seventh day. Therefore, his people were told to set aside one day to worship, remembering God's act of creation. We worship God through Jesus Christ because he reveals God the Father to us. Colossians 1:15 says, "Who is the image of the invisible God." Many people have a hard time recognizing him. He is invisible! It's hard to get to know or worship an invisible God. So people began making stuff that reminded them of some aspect of their understanding of God's character. If they thought of God as powerful, they would make an image of a bull. If they thought of God as fast, they cast him in the image of a leopard. If they thought of God as massive and unknowable, they would look up at the sun or one of the planets and worship them. If they thought of God as the great intellect, they would fashion an image of a man. The problem was that, none of these images was just right. All of them had their limitations. That's why the second of the Ten Commandments forbade the practice of making images as a representation. They could not show the full glory of God. The problem with images or pictures is that they never do justice to the original.

God had a desire for us to enter into a relationship with him, to get to know him just as he is. So when the time was right, he gave us a perfect visible image that we could look at to reveal all of God's character. The Bible talks about that image in John 1:14, "The Word became flesh and dwell among us. We beheld his glory, the glory of the only begotten of the Father, full of grace and truth." Also, in Hebrews 1:3, it says, "The Son is the radiance of God's glory and the exact representation of his being." Jesus was that perfect image. He possessed all the characteristics of God to their fullest extent because he is God. He made the invisible God visible. He revealed God to us so that we can have the opportunity to know him and choose to enter into a relationship with him. John 14:8–9 says, "Philip said unto him, Lord show us the father, and it suffice us. Jesus said unto him, have I been such a long time with you, and yet hast thou not known me Philip? He that hast seen me hast seen the Father, and how say thou, show me the father?"

God is to be worshipped as Savior. It is at the cross that we find out more about God. It is there that the promised Savior would receive the piercing, crushing, and chastisement that we deserved. God our Savior would take upon himself the iniquity of all. God our Savior would be the "Lamb of God who takes away the sin of the world" (John 1:29). There, we see him not just as the good Creator but as God the merciful and faithful and loving Savior. Our wise and powerful God came up with a plan to remain righteous, true to himself, and still forgive mankind of their sins.

Jesus Christ, the sinless Son of God, was the fulfillment of God's promise to send a Savior. The heavenly host shouts and sings in Revelation 5:8, "Worthy is the Lamb who was slain." It was our sins that carried him to the cross, drove the nails into his hands and feet, and spilled his blood. He is worthy of our worship, acknowledging the price he paid.

We worship because Jesus made it possible for us to be the objects of God's love for eternity instead of the objects of his wrath. We get what we do not deserve because Jesus Christ took upon himself what we did deserve. Not only did he die on the cross as our substitute, but he also rose from the dead three days later. And in him, we have life. That's why we praise him.

Hebrews 1:3 says, "Who being in the brightness of his glory, and the express image of his person, and upholding all things by the word of his power, when he had by himself purged out sins, sat down on the right hand of the Majesty on high."

God is to be worshipped because of his attributes. By looking at the following attributes of God, we should worship and praise him for who he is and for how much we rely on him, because he has everything in control.

First, God is omnipresent. He exists everywhere (Psalm 139:7–12). The prefix "omni" means unlimited, or all. When we say God is omnipresent it means God is everywhere at the same time. We call this omnipresence because God is free of all limitation of time and space. Therefore, he is present with us at all times. Jesus Christ promised to "never leave us nor forsake us" (Hebrews 13:5).

God is everywhere in his creation. God is present in every event, not only in every sunrise, but in every sunset and every high noon, and in every moment and in every second.

Jeremiah 23:24 says, "Do not I fill heaven and earth? saith the Lord."

Some people believe that certain places on the earth are more sacred, more filled with the presence of God than others.

In the religion of Islam, Muslims believe that God is in Mecca, Saudi Arabia, in a special way, and to worship there gives you a special charge. The Jewish religion believe that worshipping God in Jerusalem is a special place to be in God presence. But God is no more in Mecca or Jerusalem or Rome as he is everywhere else.

The omnipresence of God should remind us that we cannot hide from God when we have sinned (Psalm 139:11–12), yet we can return to him in repentance and faith. Isaiah 57:16 tells us, "For I will not contend for ever, neither will I be always wroth: for the spirit should fail before me, and the souls which I have made."

God is both far and near to us but must stay separate from us because of our sin and his holiness. Yet, he chooses to draw near to us through Jesus Christ who broke down the barrier of separation.

Second, God is omniscient. Omniscience means all-knowing. God is all-knowing in the sense that he is aware of the past, present, and future. Nothing takes him by surprise. His knowledge is total. He knows all that there is to know and all that can be known.

He knows everything (Job 37:16). Omniscient means God knows everything about everything. He knows everything about us, and yet, he loves us anyway.

God knows all things possible as well as actual because he has ordained it to come to pass according his will (Ephesians 1:11). He does not need to experience something to know about it completely.

In Psalm 139:7–8, David wrote, "Where shall I go from your Spirit? Or where shall I flee from your presence? If I ascend to heaven, you are there! If I make my bed in Sheol, you are there." When we sin and do not repent, we would like to hide our sin from God. We have the idea that if nobody saw our sin, it is not there. Yet the Bible tells us Gods knows everything, and when we sin, it may be that nobody else knows about it, but God does!

God knows everything we have ever done, yet he still loves us. He still sent his Son to die for us.

We can never escape God's attention, and just as David did, we should ask God to search us, to know our hearts, to test us, and lead us (Psalm 139:23–24). We should respond with thanks and praise, knowing that the God who knows everything is guiding us through life.

Third, God is omnipotent. Omnipotence means all-powerful. This means God can do what he wants. It means he is not subject to physical limitations like man. Being omnipotent, God has power over wind, water, gravity, physics, etc. His power is infinite, or limitless.

The word omnipotent is defined by the biblical word, "Almighty," which is never used of anyone but God. He alone is Almighty. Psalm 89:8 says, "O Lord God Almighty, who is like you? You are mighty, O Lord, and your faithfulness surrounds you."

This means God has all power and authority (Jeremiah 32:17). He can do anything. This indicates to us that his power is available to help us to become the people of God he wants us to be. He has power to accomplish his purpose for our lives (Ephesians 3:20).

We can learn to be more worshipful, trusting, and confident and at ease with God's almighty power to do whatever he pleases. David wrote in 1 Chronicles 29:1, "In your hands are strength and power to exalt and give strength to all."

God's omnipotence can clearly be seen in creation when God said, "Let there be," and it was so (Genesis 1:1–9). Man needs tools and materials to create; God simply spoke, and by the power of his word, everything was created from nothing. "By the word of the LORD were the heavens made, their starry host by the breath of his mouth" (Psalm 33:6).

God's power is exalted in us when our weaknesses are greatest because he "is able to do exceedingly, abundantly above all we can ask or think, according to the power that worketh in us" (Ephesians 3:20). It is God's power that continues to hold us in a state of grace despite our sin, and by his power, we are kept from falling (Jude 24).

Fourth, God is immutable (Malachi 3:6)! That means God is unchanging in his very being, his nature; who he is does not ever change. He is infinite and so is not subject to mutations. As he is now, he has forever been—and will forever continue to be—perfect. There was never a time when he did not exist; he will never cease to be. He is not evolving and has never evolved. He does not grow; he cannot diminish; and he is eternal, holy, pure, untainted, and perfect in every way and cannot be anything else.

God is absolute perfection. No cause for change in God exists, either in himself or outside of himself. Perfection means perfection. There is no reason for God to change because there is no change that would make him better. But man should be striving to be found complete and perfect in God's eyes.

The unchanging nature of God can give us peace. God's character will not change. He is the same yesterday, today, and forever (Hebrews 13:5). Therefore, we can trust him to be who he says he is. God is not going to suddenly stop loving us or stop being just. In our world where the only constant is change, God remains unchanged. We can rely on him to be our solid foundation.

God is to be worshipped because of his character. First, he is holy. If you are going to understand God and truly worship him, then you must understand that he is holy. To be holy literally means "apartness" or "otherness." We have come to know and to understand that holiness means "to be separated or set apart." Of all the things God is, at the center of his being, he is holy. God's holiness sets him apart from us, and our sinfulness sets us apart from him.

God is so holy the angels cried out three times in Isaiah 6:3, "Holy, Holy, Holy is the Lord." To repeat something three times means it's really important, and it is something you need to know. The angels were emphasizing the beauty of God—holy! They were emphasizing the purity of God—holy. They were emphasizing the majesty of God—holy.

God is to be worshipped because he is superior to anyone and everything in all of creation. His superiority demands that all of his creation praise him; that all of creation give him honor, reverence, and worship. Isaiah 57:15 refers to God as the "high and lofty one." He is supremely higher than all of creation—whether human beings or angelic being.

He is "high and lofty," which means he is above the problem you and I are facing; he is above our circumstances and above our situation! So it does not matter who is in the White House, or who is running the country, or what the economy does; God is in control, and that it is all for his glory.

Acceptable and Unacceptable Worship

God calls us and invites us to come and worship him. He doesn't need our worship to be God. But he delights in our worship because he is worthy of all our worship.

God has shown, in the Bible, his approval with those who follow his will as well as his displeasure with those who refuse to worship him the way he has directed. God has always been clear about how he is to be worshipped. It is man who has not always listened.

An example of acceptable and unacceptable worship in the Old Testament is that of Cain and Abel. They both worshipped God, however, Abel did as God directed, but Cain tried to worship God the way he saw fit. In Genesis 4:3–5 we read, "And in the process of time it came to pass that Cain brought an offering of fruit of the ground to the Lord. Abel also brought of the firstborn of his flock and of their fat. And the Lord respected Abel and his offering, but he did not respect Cain and his offering." Why did the Lord accept Abel's offering and reject Cain's?

Because Cain just gathered some of the harvest without bothering to see if was acceptable and presented it to the Lord. God looked into Cain's heart and knew that he didn't bring to him his best. Cain's attitude was that, "I will come and make an offering, but I will do this on my terms, not yours, Lord." When we just go through the motions, and our heart is not in our worship or what we do for the Lord, he does not accept it as worship. God told Cain that his worship would be accepted, and his service would be accepted if he would get his heart right.

Many people accept from the Bible what they like, reject the things they do not like and, at times, add things they do not like. We do not have the right to believe as we please. Anything taught or practiced by man in the field of religion which does not come from the Bible is false doctrine. Obedience requires that we do what God says to do, when God says to do it, how God says to do it, and for the reason God says to do it. If what we do in worship is not according to the word of God, then it is in vain, useless, and is unacceptable to God.

God plans for us to worship the right God. We are not called to worship the saints or to worship the building. But we are called to worship our Heavenly Father, our Holy Father, the Everlasting Father; called to worship Abba Father.

Acceptable worship gives honor and glory to God. In 1 Timothy 1:17, it says, "Now to the King eternal, immortal, invisible, to God who alone is wise be honor and glory forever and ever. Amen." The Hebrew word for glory is *kabod* meaning "weighty" or "heavy." It is that which gives a person importance and which makes a person impressive, deserving recognition and praise. Today, the word awesome would be the best word to describe the glory of God. He has awesome splendor, an awesome reputation.

The Greek word for "glory" is *doxa*, which comes from a word meaning, to form an opinion or an estimate of something or someone. Hence, to have high regard or to show respect.

Worshipper are givers! True and acceptable worship includes many things such as prayer, praise, thanksgiving, and serving God by serving others. But Paul tells us in Romans 12:1 that our supreme act of worship is to offer ourselves wholly and continually to the Lord as living sacrifices. Unless we give our body, mind, and will as a living sacrifice to God, our worship will not satisfy as it should, because we have not given as we should. A.W. Tozer said, "No man gives anything acceptable to God until he has first given himself in love and sacrifice."

The Bible also tells us to bring an offering in Psalms 96:8–9: "Give unto the Lord the glory due unto his name. Bring an offering and come into his courts. Oh, worship the Lord in the beauty his holiness; fear before him, all the earth."

Acceptable worship is the submission of all of our nature and being to God. This truth is in Psalms 51:17: "The sacrifices of God are a broken spirit: a broken and a contrite heart, O God, thou wilt not despise." Worship that is acceptable to God is all about him and not about us.

Worshipping God in Spirit and in Truth

God is not concerned with what kind of building we go to worship him, but he is concerned with HOW we worship him. He is not interested in the added special effects we put into the music or sermons, but he is interested in our hearts.

> For we are the circumcision, which worship
> God in the Spirit, and rejoice in Christ Jesus, and
> have no confidence in the flesh. (Philippians 3:3)

Spiritual worship should engage our spirit. Jesus said that God is spirit. Worship in our spirit engaging God's Spirit. He knows what is going on in your mind, the very thoughts you are thinking and feeling. So going to church is not the definition of worshipping God; it is just a small part of it. It's not just going through the motions. God is Spirit—what we need is our spirit connecting with the Holy Spirit. Our spirit is the core of who we are. It is the center of our volition and our emotions. We also know that God is a spiritual being. To worship in spirit, then, is to do something that is beyond the physical. We do not worship by simply bowing our knees; we worship through a heart posture (Psalm 51:17). And our worship is in line with the worship going on in heaven.

Jesus said in John 4:24, "But the hour cometh, and now is, when the true worshippers shall worship the Father in spirit and in truth: for the Father seeketh such to worship him."

The Father is looking for some true worshippers. When God the Father began to look for worshippers, the question is not who will worship him; but the question is, who will worship him in spirit and in truth. God is seeking worshipers who will bring him glory, not just for an hour on Sunday, but every day through all their activities. We can't properly worship God on Sundays if we're not worshiping him throughout the week.

Jesus wasn't referring to corporate worship in the sanctuary when he spoke about spiritual and truthful worship. But he was speaking about a lifestyle of worship aided by the power of the Holy Spirit that indwells the believer.

Are we really worshipping God in spirit and in truth? The word "spirit" here does not have the definite article in the original language, therefore, it is not referring to the Holy Spirit. Rather, it is referring to our own inner life, emotions, will, our heart. When we worship God in spirit, it means we worship him in our inner man, the unseen part of us—our spirit—where our principles are.

To worship God in spirit is how we connect with him, person to person. It is offering up ourselves to him in praise. Worshipping in spirit is not restricting us to one form or method, but what we feel about God must be expressed.

Worshipping God "in spirit" means to worship him with reverence, attentiveness, and having the right purpose of honoring God while comprehending what we are doing. Hebrews 12:28–29 says, "Let us have grace, by which we may serve God acceptably with reverence and godly fear. For our God is a consuming fire." Our worship must glorify God. In 1 Corinthians 6:20, it says, "For you were bought with a price; therefore glorify God in your body and in your spirit, which are God's."

In order to worship God in the right spirit, we must take time before worship to prepare our hearts and emotions so we will be in the proper frame of mind. Worshipping in spirit is authentic worship; it is when your spirit connects to God's spirit. It is deeper than the words you can form with your mouth.

What happens when a disciple worships God in the Spirit?

1. The Spirit produces life. The services will come alive. The sermons will come alive. The singing will come alive.
2. The Spirit provides liberty (2 Corinthians 3:17). The disciple worships in the Spirit to be free from the confinement of place, the commands of people, and the conformity to the past.
3. The Spirit pours out love (Romans 5:5). The disciple worships in the Spirit and will abound in love—love for the Scriptures, love for the saints, and love for sinners.

According to Psalm 89:7, "God is greatly to be feared in the assembly of the saints, and to be held in reverence by all those around him." Our worship must show great reverence toward God. He is our creator, and he holds our eternal destiny in his hands. We must strive to be pleasing to him. We are not to rush or hurry to worship, arriving late, but should always plan to be there early enough so we can be in a worshipful attitude and spirit. Our minds must be ready, attentive, and alert!

In 1 Corinthians 11:27, 29, concerning the Lord's Supper, it shows us that worship to God must be done in a manner that brings glory and honor to God and to Jesus Christ. Our thoughts during periods of worship must not be allowed to wander because the frame of mind we have plays an important role in our worship. Worship to God is holy. Our character in worship must also be holy. In 1 Peter 1:15–16, we read, "But as he who called you is holy, you also be holy in your conduct, because it is written, be holy for I am holy." Slouching over, sleeping, playing with babies, squirming, unnecessary talking, and passing notes, all show disrespect in worshipping God. Recall what Jesus says in Mark 7:6, "This people honors me with their lips, but their hearts is far from me." Active participation will get rid of our lack of interest and inattentiveness. Remember, reverence is not having a long face, folded hands, or a look of piety. Worship is a time of joy and celebration!

What does it mean to worship in truth? In truth means we are to worship the way God's word tells us. Jesus asked the Father to sanctify his disciples by his truth. "Thy word is truth" (John 17:17). We need to worship in the way prescribed in the Word of God.

In *truth* means worshiping God and him alone. In Matthew 4:10, Jesus said to him, "Away from me, Satan! For it is written, 'Worship the Lord your God, and serve him only.'"

Worship in truth involves accuracy! This means knowing what God has revealed about himself in his Word. Not just having your own idea of what God is like or what you wish He is like, but honestly searching his word to find out who he is and what he has done as Creator, and as Ruler, and as Redeemer, Savior.

Therefore, to worship God in truth is to worship him according to the truth of his Word. When it comes to the worship of God, it must be scripturally based, not founded on feelings; although feelings are God given, they are not always dependable. Our sincere feeling alone does not make our worship acceptable to God. Sometimes, we may have to worship and praise God in spite of feelings, trial, or circumstance. God has shown us in the Scriptures how to worship him. To worship in spirit and truth is not possible until you know Jesus Christ as your Lord and Savior.

If we do not worship according to God's truth, then our worship is a false worship. False worship is not only worship of false gods. It can actually be worship of the true God that is offered in ways that are out of line with the truth of God's revealed Word. It doesn't matter how sincere one is! If worship is not "in truth," sincere worship is just as unacceptable as insincere worship.

Worship Is Not for Our Entertainment

Worship is for God and God alone. Worship must be in Christ. If you are going to worship in spirit and in truth, it must be in Christ. There is an erroneous idea today that the main reason we attend worship is to "get something out of the service," rather than going there to give our worship to God. When we worship God with an attitude that is all about us, we find ourselves coming to the service focused on the music or the instruments or on who is doing the preaching. We come like judges ready to rate the event.

This is a selfish motive on our part. This is the reason people cannot be satisfied with the worship service when their emphasis is not on the proper object of worship—which should be God! We must be concerned with what God says on how he is to be worshipped instead of what we might want to offer him.

Much of our worship today has digressed to be no more than entertainment, such as choirs to sing to us and concerts to entertain us. The emphasis is on how the worship service be made more entertaining to the people to please them and not God. We have become the spectators who are being entertained. People have the roles reversed. It is God who is the spectator. Worship is not to be a spectator event; it is to be an interactive event where all in attendance participate. If we think worship is watching and listening to others worship, we are mistaken.

We are to, as Hebrews 13:15 states, "offer the sacrifice of praise to God, the fruit of our lips, giving thanks to his name." In Galatians 1:10, the question is asked, "Do I seek to please men? For if I still pleased men, I would not be a servant of Christ." Worship is God-centered not man-centered. When we seek an "emotional high" from worship and do not receive that, we are disappointed and start blaming the song, service, the preacher, etc. When we desire to have the worship service be "more entertaining," we are then failing to worship God in spirit and in truth.

As the church draws near to God, the Lord draws near to us, and we receive his grace. Entertainment cannot lead to edification. Entertainment can stir the emotions, but God uses the means of grace to change our affections. Entertainment might draw a crowd or captivate a congregation, but only the means of grace will draw people to Christ and conform them to his image.

In worship, we are the participants, not the observers. We should not worship to please and entertain ourselves.

The church doesn't need a performance of any kind to help us in our worship. We need the Word of God—read and preached, prayed and sung—for in this, we exalt and experience our God.

The *priority of worship* is "putting God first."

In the Old Testament, God's people wrestled with idolatry; they worshipped other "gods." It was a constant thing throughout the Old Testament. The people wanted to worship the gods of the people around them. It wasn't so much that they rejected worshipping their God. They wanted to worship their God and worship the other gods too. Guess what! Idolatry is with us today. It hasn't left us; it just changed forms. Anything can become a god to us—anything we worship or put an excessive amount of time into. Things that occupy our time—like money, thoughts, and attention—can take the place where God is supposed to be in our lives.

Firsts are important to God. In the first commandment (Exodus 20:5), he said, "Thou shalt have no other gods before me." God is saying in this verse, "I demand first priority in your life." What does it mean to have no other gods before him? I thought there was only one God. In this verse, we discover that the word "gods" is spelled with a lower case g. There are some little gods such as a career, sports, family, television, etc., that can crowd our affection and devotion to the true and living God.

The *purpose of worship* is "to glorify God." Revelation 4:11 says, "Thou art worthy, O Lord, to receive glory and honor and power; for thou has created all things, and for thy pleasure they are and were created."

In 1 Corinthians 6:19–20, it says, "And ye are not your own, For ye have been bought with a price: therefore glorify (exalt, lift up) God in your body." To glorify in this verse means to praise, magnify, celebrate, and honor God. It also gives the idea of getting others to acknowledge God's greatness. Since the glory of God is also the sum of all the attributes of his being, of all he has revealed of himself to man, to give God glory is to acknowledge his glory and extol it.

In the *Westminster Shorter Catechism*, the first two questions and answers are as follows.

The first question asked: "What is the chief end of man?" The answer stated was: "Man's chief end is to glorify God and to enjoy him forever."

The second question asked: "What rule hath God given to direct us how we may glorify and enjoy him?" The answer stated was: "The word of God, which is contained in the scriptures of the Old and New Testaments, is the only rule to direct us to know how we may glorify and enjoy him."

We bring glory to God by worshiping him. Worship is the primary way in which we glorify God. All of life is a reflection of whom or what we worship. We are to worship God in all that we do.

The *place of worship* is "the temple of God."

In the Old Testament, the temple was the place where men gathered to worship God. People came to the temple to give thanks and to glorify the Lord. It was a place where songs were sung, prayers were prayed, hands were raised, praise was rendered, and God was magnified. The temple was a place of worship.

However, today, our bodies are to be places where God is worshiped. In 1 Corinthians 6:19, it says, "What? Know ye not that your body is the temple of the Holy Ghost which is in you, which ye have of God and ye are not your own?" The presence of God lives inside of every believer; his presence is not centered in a building. A building is not the sanctuary; believers are his sanctuary.

The term used here for "temple" is the Greek word *nah-oss* which describes only a particular part of the Temple in Jerusalem; it was used to describe the "Holy of holies"—the place where God dwelt! Just as that temple was devoted to God as a place of worship, our bodies are to be the places where God is worshiped.

How can we worship God with our bodies?

Present your body. Paul explains how to worship the Lord in spirit and truth by adopting a lifestyle of worship. Romans 12:1–2 says, "offer our bodies as living sacrifices." The word "offer" is a technical term used to describe the bringing and presenting of an animal for sacrifice on an altar. In the Old Testament, a live animal was brought to the priest, and the owner would lay hands on the beast to symbolically say, "This animal takes my place." The animal was then killed, and the blood was sprinkled upon the altar. He challenges the believer to "offer or present your bodies as a living sacrifice, holy, and pleasing to God." In the Greek language, the word present is the term *paristemi*. It means yielding our bodies for the service of God out of free will instead of obligation; this is the first step. It means "to present once and for all" by placing oneself at the disposal of another and has the idea of relinquishing one's grip. No longer using the members of the body to do your own will but committing your body to do something for the expansion of God's Kingdom.

Paul used the term "a living sacrifice" in Romans 12:1; this was a new concept to the Jews of that day because they were used to offering dead sacrifices. Once a sacrifice is offered to God, you can't take it back. When we are called to present our "bodies" to the Lord, it means to offer our total being to him, not just bits and pieces. In 1 Corinthians 6:20, it tells us, "You were bought at a price."

The believer must covenant with God that he/she will use their body for nothing that will dishonor and degrade the Name of the Lord. Therefore, as believers, we do not have the right to do with our bodies what we wish. Jesus paid for us and is now the owner our bodies, so he says, "Hand it over; it's mine now." If we purchase something from the store, and the delivery never comes, we become upset because we paid for it, we own it, and we deserve to get it. Some believers have never truly handed their bodies to the Lord Jesus Christ, although they have considered themselves to be Christians for years. God deserves the right to your body.

Praise him continually. "Let us continually offer the sacrifice of praise to God" (Hebrews 13:15). The writer of Hebrews is saying that praising God shouldn't be a time set aside on Sunday for just an hour or two. We shouldn't limit our praise to God to a once-a-week optional exercise. Praise is too important for that. True praise is an everyday event. Therefore, we must make a conscious decision and effort to praise him continually! Determine in our hearts that we will not allow the circumstances of life to stop us from giving praise to the Lord.

Practice his presence. Hebrews 13:5 reminds us that Jesus is always with us. So we must walk in the knowledge of his abiding presence. The Lord is teaching us confidence in him. He is revealing himself as our *helper* so that we do not give in to our fears, but rather, learn more fully how to trust him. If you will realize that Jesus is always there, and he is watching, it may prevent you from engaging in activities that would dishonor his name.

Establish kingdom priorities. Matthew 6:33 says, "But seek first His kingdom and His righteousness and all these things will be added to you." This indicates that we must forfeit all other priorities and exalt the Lord Jesus. Kingdom speaks of the rule and reign of Christ in all of our life. His kingdom speaks of Jesus having the proper place in your life.

Public and Private Worship

Worship happens in two spheres: public and private, therefore, a disciple is expected to worship the Lord both publicly and privately. Public worship occurs when the people of God assemble for the express purpose of giving to the Lord the glory due his name and enjoying the joy of his promised special presence with his own people. This kind of worship is sometimes called "corporate worship" (because the body of Christ, that is, the church, is collectively involved in this encounter with God), and sometimes, it is called "gathered," "assembled," or "congregational" worship. This important aspect of worship is featured in both the Old and New Testaments. While Psalm 100:2 and Hebrews 10:25 speak of "coming before the Lord" and "assembling together," they are both addressing public worship.

Public worship helps the believer to recognize that he/she is not an only child in the kingdom but is part of a bigger family. The Bible tells us in Hebrews 10:23–25, "Let us hold fast the profession of our faith without wavering; (for he is faithful that promised;)And let us consider one another to provoke unto love and to good works: Not forsaking the assembling of ourselves together, as the manner of some is; but exhorting one another: and so much the more, as ye see the day approaching."

The words "assembling together" means that Christians are to gather together with other believers for the express purpose of worship. We draw near to the Lord Jesus Christ! We do not come to church, primarily, to hear a sermon, to listen to music, to fellowship with others, or to give an offering. The overriding purpose of our coming together is to draw near to Jesus. Today, many Christians are heard saying, "I don't have to attend church to worship God." It is true that Christians ought to worship Christ alone; but public worship is taught in the Bible, and together, as the body of Christ, we are commanded to draw near to him.

The New Testament describes the church as a "body," a "building," and a "family." Each one of these terms speaks of the relationship between the individual units and that of the whole. We are individually Christian, but collectively, we are Christians too.

There is something special about gathering publicly and praising God together! Peter reminds us in 1 Peter 2:9, that God has brought Jew and Gentile together into the church. Now, he says, "But ye are a chosen generation, a royal priesthood, an holy nation, a peculiar people; that ye should shew forth the praises of him who hath called you out of darkness into his marvelous light."

We gather in public worship for communion and baptism which was given to the church by the Lord Jesus Christ so we can celebrate, remember, and proclaim who he is and what he has done in our lives with the people he has placed in our lives.

Another reason that we assemble together is "to stimulate one another to love and good deeds." Our assembling together is an act of encouragement to other believers. We should always seek ways to encourage one another, and worshiping together is one of those ways. We must worship God with other believers and in private as well. Public worship should be an outward reflection of what God is doing in our hearts. Therefore, when we come together and let the inside come to the outside, others in the congregation are exhorted or challenged to strengthen their own walk with the Lord. That's why we should never be ashamed to show everything we have into our public worship. You never know who needs that encouragement.

When we sing together on Sunday morning or read Scripture together or pray together, we are communicating not only to God but also to one another. The Apostle Paul said in Ephesians 5:19, "Speaking to yourselves in psalms and hymns and spiritual songs, singing and making melody in your heart to the Lord."

When we come together in public or corporate worship on Sunday morning, we get a picture of what heaven is like.

Private worship, which is sometimes called "secret worship" or "personal worship," is taught and seen throughout Scripture, especially by Jesus. Every believer needs to have personal worship time, just as every human being needs to eat, drink, and sleep each day. You can go without those things for a little while, but pretty soon, you will get sick, and eventually, die. In the same way, neglecting our *personal worship time with God,* literally, takes away spiritual life from our souls.

The way we meet God in the altar of our hearts is to find a quiet place where we can spend time alone with him. I call this "private or personal worship time." Jesus gave us an example of this in Mark 1:35, "And in the morning, rising up a great while before day, he went out, and departed into a solitary place, and there prayed."

Private worship demonstrates that worship is in you because the Spirit of God indwells you. Psalm 113:3 says, "From the rising of the sun unto the going down of the same the Lord's name is to be praised." Praise and worship should be the daily routine of the disciple's life. God wants us to worship both privately and publicly with the body of believers. Any believer who worships privately will have no problem worshiping publicly with other believers.

When we acknowledge that we are to "worship in spirit and in truth," we are saying that in public, private, and all of life, we are to glorify and enjoy God.

PART 2

Equipping the Saints

And he gave some, apostles; and some, prophets; and some, evangelists; and some, pastors and teachers;

For the perfecting of the saints, for the work of the ministry, for the edifying of the body of Christ:

Till we all come in the unity of the faith, and of the knowledge of the Son of God, unto a perfect man, unto the measure of the stature of the fullness of Christ:

That we henceforth be no more children, tossed to and fro, and carried about with every wind of doctrine, by the sleight of men, and cunning craftiness, whereby they lie in wait to deceive;

But speaking the truth in love, may grow up into him in all things, which is the head, even Christ:

From whom the whole body fitly joined together and compacted by that which every joint supplieth, according to the effectual working in the measure of every part, maketh increase of the body unto the edifying of itself in love. (Ephesians 4:11–16, KJV)

Equipping the Saints
through the Word

God has equipped his family to take care of his business. He has given us a clear plan, an exciting purpose, and an effective method! Ephesians 4:11 tells us, Jesus Christ gave the gifts.

He gave the five-fold ministries to his church. The gifts are not the persons, but the gift is Jesus Christ himself within those persons. These gifts are performing all of this work as they proceed from Christ.

Ephesians 4:7 says, "But unto every one of us is given grace according to the measure of the gift of Christ." Grace literally means free gift. In fact, God could give to his people no greater gift, so he gave us of himself. He chooses to do it through apostles, prophets, evangelists, pastors, and teachers. He chooses not to use those who send themselves or those who are sent by men. Therefore, we can see that it is not gifted people who do any of this work, but rather the Gift Himself does the work through them.

In the original Greek, the word equip is *katartismon* from which we get our English word "artisan"—an artist or craftsman, someone who works with his hands to make or build things. It is a special point of interest that this word first appears in the New Testament in connection with the calling of the disciples.

Equipping also means "to prepare" and "to strengthen." It gives the idea of preparing someone for a job or rendering someone functional. Preparation is essential for discipleship.

The word for equipping usually means fixing something that's broken, such as when Peter, James, and John were mending their torn nets (Matthew 4:21), or it is supplying something that is lacking as in 1 Thessalonians 3:10: "We desire to supply, or equip, what is lacking in your faith." The Lord Jesus Christ gave leaders to the church whose job is to repair what's broken and supply what's lacking in the believers.

So we can see that the word "equipping" carries the idea of RES-TORATION; that is, to mend what has been broken, or to repair. It carries the idea of PREPARATION—to fit out, to put in order, arrange or adjust. It also carries the idea of COMPLETION (or perfection)—to make one what he or she ought to be. So when gifted leaders prepare the believers for the works of service, they restore them back to usefulness, deal with the sins that would hinder their service, then prepare them or train them so that they would be fruitful for God. That's what it means to equip or to prepare God's people for service.

In Ephesians 4:11, the apostles, prophets, evangelists, pastors, and teachers are gifts given to the church to equip others to do the ministry, not to just keep doing the work themselves. The evangelist is not called to reach the lost but to equip the saints to reach the lost. The teacher is not called to simply teach the saints but to equip the saints to teach. The true teacher is the person that has reached a level of maturity and instruct the next generation of believers how to teach. The officers of the church are given to equip the church so that the saints—everybody in the congregation who has been saved by Jesus Christ—together can fulfill the work of service and the building up of the body.

The Apostle John laid out three phases of maturing that are helpful for us. He refers to little children, young men, and fathers (1 John 2:12–14). These categories can help to understand the maturing process.

Little children cannot help themselves but are consumed with their own needs. That is the nature of immaturity. In the spiritual life, young believers are focused on themselves and their own spiritual needs. They typically are wracked with shame over their sin. The good news for them, according to 1 John 2:12, "your sins are forgiven." The child is set free from their sins, and most of their childhood will really be about coming to realize this important truth.

Young men are warriors that finally venture out into adulthood, according to 1 John 2:14. This phase of development is where leaders begin to emerge and take on the issues of life. Young men are interested mostly in winning the battle and wooing the girl. Therefore, he is no longer only thinking of himself but is now facing an enemy. The good news for them, according to John is, "You have overcome the evil one."

Fathers (1 John 2:13–14) are a phase of reproduction. It is a time of maturing when you now are more concerned with the success of your children than your own success. Your life, at this point, is spent to help others to grow and bear fruit. No longer are fathers the ones taking on the enemy with a full frontal assault, instead, they are training the new, young warriors with their own rich experience and mature paternal heart. The good news for these leaders is, "You know the Father." Intimacy with God is the reward to maturity and is actually a far greater reward than large attendance and celebrity status. It is my opinion that this "father phase" is when we become true equippers of others. Not enough Christian leaders reach the "father phase" of maturation, which is unfortunate in so many ways.

"The work of ministry" in Ephesians 4:12 is not a reference to a church office. It translates *diakonias*, meaning "service." The most literal definition of the word "ministry" is "waiting on tables." It's a reference to humble service.

The church is healthy only when it is filled with people who serve, when gifted leaders equip the gifted, and God's people use their gifts to do the difficult work of serving others. Church leaders are one of Christ's gifts to the church.

The Word of God must be taught in such a way that it is real and can be applied to the daily lives of people. The believer must be taught, not just in the basics of the faith, but also in how to be Christians in their families, work, and relationships. They must be taught how to be effective Christians and how to live their lives to the glory of God!

The Cost of Discipleship

The Christian life can be described as a journey. It begins when we respond to God's call of salvation, and we accept His Son Jesus Christ as Lord and Savior of our lives. The goal of this journey is to grow into Christlikeness, becoming spiritually mature. But as we travel along the way in this journey, we can experience delays, detours, discouragement, and dangers.

Many Christians today have made a verbal commitment to follow the Lord with their whole hearts, but after encountering dangers, delays, discouragements, and detours, that commitment has faded. To make progress in our spiritual journey, we must not stop short of complete commitment to God. Jesus said in Luke 9:23, "If any man will come after me, let him deny himself, and take up his cross daily, and follow me."

Discipleship has a cost; it requires commitment and consistency to follow Jesus. The original disciples left their families and good jobs. James and John left their father Zebedee's fishing business to follow Jesus. Matthew left his tax collecting table to follow Jesus.

The Gospel of Luke has some helpful insights about "the cost of discipleship." Luke 9:23 says, "And he said to them all, if any man will come after me, let him deny himself, and take up his cross daily, and follow me." In this verse, Jesus is very clear: if you want to be his disciple, you must forsake or deny yourself. You must put his interests above your interest and know that he is in the driver's seat, not you.

The first cost to discipleship is the denial of self. The Greek word "deny" literally means to "disregard your own interest or to act entirely unlike yourself." The King James "translation" use the word "deny," but some paraphrases may offer an easier to understand picture. Such as, "ignore yourself", "say no to the things you want," "must put aside his own desires and conveniences," and "has to let me lead," "You're not in the driver's seat." All these statements lead to Jesus Christ's call for "self-denial."

Denying yourself may include denying things that you desire, but it is really telling those who follow Jesus Christ to deny themselves as their own lord. It is telling us to say no to the god that is me. "I do not know Lord me, I do not obey Lord me, and I do not bow down to the god called me."

Self, meaning our ego or our pride, is a strong force that must be brought under the control of truth and faith (1 Corinthians 9:24–27). Our desires (intentions, resolve, purposes, and determination) must all line up in agreement with the will of God. We must put away everything that keeps us from following Jesus.

If we don't deny ourselves, then we will raise our own status to the level of God. The worship, honor, praise, glory, trust, and more that we should offer God, we will give to self. To really be a disciple of Jesus Christ means that "self" is no longer on the throne of your life—Jesus is your Lord!

The second cost of discipleship is death. Another cost of following Christ in this world is the cross that he will give you to bear. Taking up the cross symbolizes suffering and shame, surrender and death. To be a disciple of Jesus Christ, one must lose his/her life for Christ's sake. Every follower of Christ must daily crucify himself and live for Christ by faith. The Apostle Paul understood well what this meant, and he lived it out day by day (Galatians 2:20).

In Luke 9:23, the same term was used by the Roman soldier when he commands Simon of Cyrene to pick up Jesus's cross and carry it to Calvary. It is speaking directly to bearing the cross of death. Jesus understood that he was about to have to, literally, bear a cross and die for the sin of the world. He also wanted all who were to follow him to understand that they, too, would have to be willing to face the same thing, and face it with the same willing attitude in their heart. One of the old hymns written by Thomas Shepherd relates to this idea; it says, "Must Jesus bear the cross alone and all the world go free, no there is a cross for everyone and there is a cross for me."

Jesus had to bear, but what a good result came from it. Isaiah 53:10 says, "Yet it pleased the Lord to bruise him; he hath put him to grief: when thou shalt make his soul an offering for sin, he shall see his seed, he shall prolong his days, and the pleasure of the Lord shall prosper in his hand."

Because Jesus suffered on the cross, all the world can be blessed with salvation by faith (Ephesians 2:8–9). Good came out of evil. Blessing and benefit came from suffering and sorrow. When God's people suffer, something good is going come out of it as a result. That is the promise of Romans 8:28: "And we know that all things work together for good to them that love God and to them that are the called according to his purpose."

As a disciple of Jesus, as a follower of Christ, he is calling you to DIE! Dietrich Bonhoeffer's book, *The Cost of Discipleship*, tells us what God requires according to the Bible, and Dietrich Bonhoeffer says, "When Christ calls a man, He bids him come and die." To give ALL of who he is and be willing to die for the cause and sake of Christ!

The third cost of discipleship is determination. A disciple who decides to follow Jesus must be determined to walk along with him wherever he leads. Every disciple is to deny himself or herself and pick up his/her cross at the beginning of each day, in order to continue following Jesus throughout the day.

This is a picture of a person who has been found guilty of a crime and is sentenced to death. That person is forced to carry a cross upon which he/she is to be crucified.

Taking up your cross is not a round trip; there is no return ticket on this journey because it is a one-way trip.

If you are going to follow Jesus, you are going to have to leave some things behind. Peter and Andrew left their fishing nets; James and John left their father; Matthew left his job as a tax collector.

If you are ever going to have the type of relationship you truly need with the Lord Jesus, there are some things you have got to say goodbye to. You must purpose in your heart to follow Jesus. Following him must become your one true objective in life. This is the one thing that determines all that you are and all that you do.

The Yoke

The yoke, just like the cross, is a wooden symbol of the Christian experience. The cross speaks of leaving the world for Christ; "Take up thy cross and follow me." The yoke speaks of learning in the world from Christ: "Take my yoke upon you and learn of me." The cross speaks of sacrifice; the yoke speaks service. The disciple must bear both; he or she cannot choose to take one and leave the other out.

Matthew 11:28–30 says, "Come unto me, all ye that labor and are heavy laden, and I will give you rest. Take my yoke upon you, and learn of me; for I am meek and lowly in heart: and ye shall find rest unto your souls. For my yoke is easy, and my burden is light."

Used as a verb, "yoke" means to join or to unite. It was used frequently in the Old Testament—it can mean something more severe such as to force into labor or bondage, like a beast of burden, or worse, as a slave.

Yokes were common in Jesus's day. Yokes were placed on oxen so that the animals could work together as a team and not be hurt by the burden they carried. In the example of the ox, the older and stronger ox was able to take the load off of the young and inexperienced ox. He was able to bear the weight of the work because the yoke transferred that weight from the smaller, weaker ox to the larger, stronger ox.

By working as a team, the two ox are able to share the load that they bear. When one slips, the other can pick up the weight, and they can continue on. If the weight is too much for one, the other can pick up the slack, and they can continue forward.

Just like the younger ox was able to transfer his concerns to the older ox, we, too, can transfer our concerns from ourselves—the weaker—to the stronger back of Jesus. We can rest in the strength of Jesus as he carries through the burdens of our life.

When we stumble, he's there to pick up our burdens. When the weight on our shoulders is too much for us to bear, he's there to pick us up and allow us to continue on the journey together. When we have no place else to turn, he's there to support us in our time of need.

In New Testament times, the phrase, "to take the yoke of" was used by rabbi's to refer to "becoming a submitted disciple of a teacher." Yokes aren't used much in our modern world today. It is a wooden harness used to guide oxen or other draft animals while plowing fields. The yoke still exists in some developing countries and within more traditional cultures, but by and large, it has been replaced by tractors or other mechanized equipment.

In the Bible, it is figuratively used as a symbol of slavery (1 Timothy 6:1); servanthood: "I broke the bars of your yoke and enabled you to walk with heads held high" (Leviticus 26:13). Also, in Jeremiah 27:8–12, it's a symbol of submission, forced subjection; burden, load of oppression in Isaiah 9:4; bondage to sin in Lamentations 1:14: "My sins have been bound into a yoke, by his hands, they were woven together."

The plowman binds the yoke upon the neck of the oxen so that it would not fall off or be shaken off. Yoke bound around the neck of man would cause his strength to diminish; one may waver and fall under the load of yoke.

The yoke of Jesus gives a picture of three things for his followers:

1. *Connection.* "Be with me." Yokes are made for two, not one. We were not meant to go through life living apart from God. His yoke fits well and is lighter than the one were pulling by ourselves. Be connected to Jesus! By taking the yoke of Jesus and submitting to his lead, we allow him to bear the weight of our burdens. When you are yoked to Jesus, your burdens are not removed, but Jesus is your yoke-

mate, and he is pulling with you. He has fit you with a yoke that is perfectly made for you and him to work together.

2. *Direction.* "Follow me." The idea of a yoke pictures the forward motion of two connected together. The yoke allows us to submit to Jesus's lead. You cannot be yoked to Jesus and go your own way anymore. But being yoked to Jesus allows him to direct our path. We follow him and his direction for our life. Follow Jesus!

3. *Cooperation.* "Work with me." To be yoked together means that we cooperate with his work. Before we come to him, we were living for this side of eternity. Now we are joined to his work and discover that our lives make an eternal impact. We experience this only when we obey his command: "Take my yoke upon you and learn of me."

The Disciple's Help

The development of a disciple is the work of the Holy Spirit. The Holy Spirit has been given to us to help us learn how to live the new life we have in Christ. It is the power of the Holy Spirit dwelling within us; we can learn how to live life a whole new way. Paul said in Philippians 2:12, "Continue to work out your salvation with fear and trembling, for it is God who works in you to will and to act according to his good purpose."

The Holy Spirit is God with us, helping and empowering us to live a life that displays the goodness of God. As the flesh fights for control, it is the Spirit that steps in and helps us to be who God created us to be. Believers can start each day knowing the Holy Spirit is there to help them. He is the power that sustains, energizes, and keeps us on a holy path.

The Holy Spirit helps the disciple in the process of sanctification: to die to the old self and to become free from the entanglement of sin and live a victorious life. Paul said in 1 Corinthians 6:11, "But you were washed, you were sanctified, you were justified in the name of the Lord Jesus Christ and by the Spirit of our God." The word *sanctified* means to be set apart as sacred. It is the purification of sin and spiritual maturing to help us become more Christlike. This is an important process for a believer; it is leaving behind the old life and becoming a new person in Christ. But it's a daily process, and it takes time.

The goal of the disciple and every believer is Christlikeness, and this can only take place through the power of the Holy Spirit. This is being transformed into the image of Jesus Christ (Romans 8:29).

The Disciple's Faith

Everything that God demands in discipleship can be summed up in one word—faith. Faith is our response to God's offer of salvation and abundant life. Because of his grace, God makes his spiritual riches available to us, but it is only through faith we can accept them. Everything we receive in the Christian life is by faith. Our faith is what allows us to lay claim on all that God has promised.

In discipleship, the amount of our faith is not as important as the object of our faith. Faith is only as good as its object. The object of our faith is not the church, it is not a creed, and it is not a book. But it is "faith toward our Lord Jesus Christ" (Acts 20:21).

Faith begins with a knowledge of God's word. A disciple must know the word of God in order to have faith. Romans 10:17 say, "So then, faith cometh by hearing, and hearing by the word of God."

We will face many obstacles to our faith. But as we encounter situations that cause us to question God's involvement in our lives, we must trust him and not waver. One of the hindrances we experience in our lives is "living by sight." It has been said that seeing is believing; but the Lord usually does not give us visual evidence of his activity. We must trust him even when we don't see him working.

Neglecting the Word of God will hinder our faith. Daily meditation upon Scripture is absolutely vital to our faith. The Word of God reminds us of how he has helped others in the past. If we neglect to read the Word, then our confidence in the Lord will surely falter.

Another hindrance to our faith is when we continue in sin. When we insist on holding on to sinful habits and behaviors, we lose the ability to believe God for all he wants to do in our lives. This sin short-circuits our faith and distracts us from our relationship with the Father.

The tactics Satan will use also hinder us in our faith. Satan will do whatever he can to stop our devotion to the Lord. He will always suggest to us that God will not do as he has promised. But we must never believe the devil's lies.

The feelings of guilt will hinder our faith. The regrets of past sins can keep us from fully trusting the Lord. Believing ourselves unworthy of his love, we can doubt his favor and his promise to work in our lives. But we must always remember, the Father forgives us on the basis of Jesus Christ's shed blood on the cross, not by our own merit.

A description of faith (Hebrews 11:1–3)

Faith is best described in Hebrews 11:1: "Now faith is the substance of things hope, the evidence of things not seen." First, "Faith is the substance of things hoped for." The meaning of the word "substance" means that faith gives support to that which we hope for. It's like a "title deed" that guarantees the promise will be fulfilled.

The word "substance" can also translate "confidence" or that which has a foundation. The Amplified Bible says in Hebrews 11:1, "Now faith is the assurance (the confirmation, the title deed) of the things (we) hope for, being the proof of things (we) do not see and the conviction of their reality (faith perceiving as real fact what is not revealed to the senses)."

Second, faith is the "evidence of things not seen." The word "evidence" can be translated as "proof." Faith is proof of the reality we cannot see with our physical eyes. Though we cannot see God, we believe that he is and that he rewards those who diligently seek him (Hebrews 11:6).

Christians believe in those things that the physical eye cannot see. We haven't seen Jesus, but we believe. We haven't seen the victory, but we believe it has been won. Faith is trusting in what Jesus did on the cross as sufficient for our salvation.

The product of the Gospel in the life of the believer is "righteousness." Man has two great problems. He thinks he is righteous and is, therefore, acceptable to the Lord. Man is not righteous and cannot produce righteousness by self-will or his own works.

Paul writes in Romans 1:17, "For in it the righteousness of God is revealed from faith to faith; as it is written." The means of righteousness or salvation is not of works, good deeds, or moral life. If so, a man would earn his righteousness on his own, and it would not be a righteousness of God but of himself. The righteousness of God is holiness and perfection infinitely higher than the righteous works of sinful man which are as filthy rags in God's eyes. Thus, God's righteousness must be obtained by faith.

But the just (righteous) shall live by faith. The emphasis in this verse is on the manner in which the believer obtains salvation, and that is "by faith in the gospel," Salvation and God's righteousness go hand in hand. The indication is not only on the fact that God saves, but also on the fact that he does so righteously.

The phrase "from faith to faith" refers to the fact that the believer's life is to be one of faith in God. It means that faith is the beginning of the salvation process, and it is also goal. When a person first exercises faith in the Lord Jesus Christ, that person is saved from the penalty of sin and declared righteous. As the believer lives by faith, God continues to save him or her from the power of sin in order to live and do everything right. It reveals a righteousness of God resulting from faith (out of faith), which is offered to those who believe (unto faith). As the believer's life is lived in faith day by day, the righteousness of God is revealed in the believer's life from "beginning faith" to "ending faith." Faith is to be the way of life for the child of God.

That also means your faith must be accompanied by action; else, it has no life (see James 2:17). It is not faith at all. It doesn't have the power to change a single individual, let alone the world.

The first faith in this verse speaks of faith that causes you to act; faith that calls out to God and allow him to take control of your life when you submit and surrender your life to him.

The second faith in Romans 1:17 is power-giving faith. Faith that causes you to act. The faith that causes you to live in a relationship with God.

The first faith saves you. "For by grace are ye saved through faith; and that not of yourselves: it is the gift of God" (Ephesians 2:8). The second one identifies you as a child of God. The first faith is all about assurance; and the second tells you what you can become. The first faith deals with redemption, and the second deals with risk. The first faith is a gift, and the second is all about growth.

Once a person becomes saved and righteous by faith in God, that person will begin to live a daily a life of faith. Just as it stands written, "The just shall live by faith" (Romans 1:17). This righteousness is based on faith and leads us into an ever increasing walk of faith.

The Disciple and Church Membership

In today's society, many Christians see no need to belong to a local church. Membership in a local congregation is not automatic; it is must be sought out by an individual. The local church is made up of Christians in one location who agree to work together. Membership has its privileges, but it also has its obligations, such as, to bear one another's burdens, to exhort one another, to assemble together, and to serve one another with whatever abilities we have, etc.

Why is it that so many people lack the desire to become members of the local churches they're already attending? Part of the reason for a lack of interest in church membership is the commitment phobia of our culture and always waiting for a better deal to come along. Most people in our generation treat the church like it is expendable. Their commitment to the church is conditioned on their schedules, their routines, their convenience, or their desires of the moment. There is no real commitment to the mission of the church, the worship of the church, the outreach of the church, or the needs of the church. Today's local church is afflicted with a "take it or leave it" attitude.

When you join a church, you are not joining a social club; you are publicly declaring your faith in Jesus and joining yourself to a group of Christians in life and mission. Every believer should make a personal commitment to a local church to have a strong, growing relationship with the people of God, where you can encourage each other in Christ and pray for one another and bear each other's burdens.

According to Ephesians 5:25, the church is the bride of Christ. The image of the bride tells us deep things about the devotion and love of Christ Jesus for us, his bride. So how can a believer love the groom (Jesus Christ) and hate his bride (the church)? In Ephesians 5:30, the church is called the *body* of Christ, and we are members of his body. How can a believer love the *head* (Jesus Christ) and hate his body (the church)?

The church is a community of the baptized believers. In the New Testament, baptism is the sign of personal faith in Jesus. So only those who have been baptized as believers can be members

The pattern throughout the New Testament was for pastors to oversee the local body of believers. Their duties clearly defined a group of members who were under their care. Every local church should view membership as discipleship and implement a member-ship process. Instead of making it easy to join your church, make the process more involved. The church should ensure that membership actually means something for members. Identify the unique privi-leges, roles, and responsibilities that members have in your church.

God makes us a part of his larger family when we become born again. Then we should covenant within a local body and live in com-munity with them, agreeing to live by godly principles and stan-dards. Church membership doesn't save us. But it does enable us to grow and become spiritually mature in Christ. Church membership should be a commitment to helping the membership to progress in discipleship, moving every member into spiritual maturity and active ministries for which they are gifted. A Christian that is not a member of a local church is like a soldier without an army or a baseball player without a team. He or she will not get very far in fulfilling their call-ing and purpose.

Jesus Christ loves the local church, because the local church is the main instrument through which he administers his grace to the believers. In John 10:14, Jesus identified his followers as sheep, and sheep need a shepherd. It is a natural thing for a sheep to go astray, therefore a sheep needs a shepherd to lead him. Sheep need to be led to food and water. Sheep need a shepherd for provision. Sheep are helpless prey to the wolves. Sheep need a shepherd for protection. A pastor is a shepherd. Pastors are commanded to "feed the flock of God—taking the oversight—being examples to the flock" (1 Peter 5:2, 3). Being a member of a local body allows the believer to have a pastor (shepherd) to feed them and have oversight over them and be an example to them."

Church membership is making a public vow that you are a follower of Jesus Christ and you will live as a follower of Christ. You will also be committed to serve and support the church family, and will come under the direction and the correction or discipline of the leadership of that church body.

In 1 Corinthians 12:12–31, Paul says the church is a body. The phrase that he uses in 1 Corinthians 12:12 to describe the individual connectedness is we are "members of the body." Being a member means you have taken a step of commitment to the church and identifies with the church family. This is a meaningful way of obeying Jesus' command for us to love one another. It means that you have shown you are committed to the whole church, not just your group of friends. It also means that you know that the other church members are committed to you in Christian love.

Disciples who are not members of the church in which they attend feel no obligation to that local church. It is not their church, and they really couldn't care less. Even though they attend regularly, they seldom get involved. They come for what they can get rather than what they can give to help build a strong and effective local church. Every disciple should be encouraged to invest themselves in a local church.

A disciple should belong to a local church by becoming a member, expressing their agreement with the teaching of the church that they are joining. They should commit to supporting the church financially and vow to protect the unity of the local congregation. Also, show willingness and availability to use their gifts in the church and to pursue the growth of the local church.

They must not hide their light under a bushel but put to use what God has given them. How terrible that a hand or foot is not working in the body of Christ. Jesus said, "I will build my church." The talents and abilities of every believer can be used for the Lord in His church.

A disciple need the local church and what it offers. When you go to church to worship, you are proclaiming your faith in a risen Lord. You are teaching your children the importance of God's house. You are building a wall of protection around your heart and life. You are strengthening your faith and growing in the Lord.

Hebrews 10:25–26 says, "Not forsaking the assembling of ourselves together, as the manner of some is." This tells us that church attendance is not an optional matter; it is a command from the Lord. An absence from church is a vote to close the doors! It is a testimony to the world that your life is more important than his worship.

As a disciple and member of a church, you are responsible for protecting the gospel and the gospel's ministry in your church by helping to disciple other church members. Paul says in Ephesians 4:25, "Speak every man truth with his neighbor, for we are members of one of another." Speak truth to them and help them to grow. Our words should be "good for building up someone in need." Basic discipleship involves building up other believers. It is a part of fulfilling the Great Commission and making disciples.

The Equipping Gifts to the Church

These gifts are given to build up the church, to help the church realize its full potential value and its mission. The gifts are not given for personal enhancement.

Christ has given every believer a gift or gifts—the ability to be able to serve the Lord in a special way. Ephesians 4:7 says, "But unto every one of us is given grace according to the measure of the gift of Christ." The word grace in this context means gift. So each of us has been given a gift, and every member in the church is charged with using their gift. But just because we have a supernatural ability to serve, it doesn't mean we can do it automatically. It takes some training and preparation. It takes instructions and development under the oversight of godly leaders. That's why Jesus Christ gave the church gifted leaders. We must learn how to use the gifts we have been given.

*****

The following group of gifted leaders were given to the church to equip for service:

Apostle or apostolos. (*apo*: from, and *stello*: to send) Meaning, one who is sent forth as a messenger and should not be confused with a disciple (who is a follower, servant, or student who learns from a teacher). Traditionally, Jesus had twelve apostles who spread the gospel after his resurrection. An apostle was an eyewitness to the physical ministry of Jesus Christ, and therefore, apostles do not exist today. Paul was considered an apostle because he had seen the risen

Christ. Jesus equipped these people to set up the church. The church has been set up (Ephesians 2:20) built on the foundation of the apostles and prophets, with Christ Jesus himself as the chief cornerstone. Today, missionaries may be viewed also as one who is sent, however, they are not to be considered apostles.

Prophet, Ro'eh, hozeh. ("seer," *Navi*: prophet) One called to speak. Is an individual who is claimed to have been contacted by the supernatural or the Divine and serves as an intermediary with humanity, delivering this newfound knowledge from the supernatural entity to other people. The message that the prophet conveys is called a prophecy. The main mission of a prophet was to be the mouthpiece for God. The position of prophet is also not for today, however, there are many who are prophets in the sense that they "forth tell" the Word of God like the prophets of old.

The offices of the apostles and the prophets have already ceased to a certain extent. Paul writes in Ephesians 3:20 and tell us that the church is "built on the foundation of the apostles and prophets, with Christ Jesus himself as the chief cornerstone." We lay the foundation at the beginning of the construction of a building. So, being foundational, the apostles and the prophets were needed at the early stage of the church in its history.

Evangelist or euangelistes. (*eu*: well; *angelous*: messenger, a messenger of God) Preacher of the gospel. *Evangelizo*: proclaim glad tidings. *Evangelion*: good news, gospel. A believer who proclaims Jesus Christ to nonbelievers and, thereby, participates in evangelism. Missionaries are evangelists, being, essentially, preachers of the gospel. Not every Christian has the gift of evangelism, but all Christians share the role of witnessing. All Christians, regardless of their individual gifts, have their God-given places in the evangelism of the church. The biblical position of an evangelist is more like a church planter today or the preacher.

Pastor or poimen. A shepherd, one who tends herds or flocks. They nourish, protect, and care for the church (the believers). Some carry the title "elder," and there are some who shepherd the flock who do not have that title. No matter what the trappings of titles or positions, there are some who, by God's grace, naturally shepherd the flock. Christian pastors usually refers to an *ordained* leader of a Christian congregation. The term "pastor" is also related to the role of elder, overseer, or bishop within the New Testament but is not synonymous with the biblical understanding of minister. Minister: Hebrew is *sharat* meaning to wait on or serve.

Teacher. (*Didaskalos*: teacher; *kalodidaskalos*: teacher of what is good. A person who teaches or instructs.

These gifts were given to men, and the gifted men were given to the church. Why? So that the church can begin to grow and come into the stature of the fullness of Christ. They are the equippers given to equip the church.

The first part of Ephesians 4 verse 11 says, "And he gave some... to pastors and teachers; to prepare God's people." The word "prepare" is the same word used to describe what James and John were doing when they were "preparing" their nets in Matthew 4:21. That means, they had to clean all the seaweed off them, stitch up the sections that were torn, untangle them, and get them ready to be used again at a moment's notice. The nets were prepared for service, not for storage. In classical Greek, the word was used of the setting of a bone in order to put it back into proper alignment in the body. Pastors are to repair what's broken and supply what's missing so the saints can be strengthened to serve.

Servants, *serve!* Look at the next phrase in verse 12: "for works of service." The preposition translated "for" is really the word "into." Those who are equipped go into ministry. The work of service is ministry. The words here mean to do the work of a servant. This particular work done varies with the particular gifts the believer has received from God, but all of it together makes up the work God has given to his Church. The work of the church is done by the people of the church. We mistakenly speak of only pastors or missionaries, even paid staff, as those who go into the ministry. Every member of the family of God is a minister, and every saint is a servant. In 1 Peter 4:10, it says, "Each one should use whatever gift he has received to serve others, faithfully administering God's grace in its various forms."

The work of ministry belongs to all the saints, and Paul describes that work as "building up the body of Christ." The work God has given us to do is to build up the body of Christ by fulfilling the Great Commission, with everyone doing their part.

The body of Christ is built up numerically as disciples are made. People come to salvation and join in as part of the church. The body of Christ grows in maturity as each Christian is taught to "observe all that [Jesus] has commanded."

The Gifts Help Lead to Growth

I remember a car I drove for years that needed a front-end alignment. The car pulled to the right so badly, I drove straddling the center line to keep from going off the road. This reminds me of many believers who are out of line and are pulling to the left or to the right of God's Word.

The Word of God is God's alignment tool. It is his perfect standard, and the gifted leaders' job is to make sure that every believer understands that he or she must be adjusted according to God's Word; not changing the Word to adjust to their likes and dislikes.

According to Ephesians 4:12–15, the gifts lead to growth in at least six ways:

The body is built up. "So that the body of Christ may be built up." The two words "so that" refer to the purpose behind serving—so that the body is built up. Spiritual gifts are not toys to play with but tools to build with. Or, to paraphrase our mission statement, once we are equipped and serving, we will become growing and faithful disciples (followers).

The words built up comes from the Greek word *oikodome*. It means the building of a house. It is the word "edify" which is a construction term that was used to describe a building going up brick by brick or the process of making a structure stronger to improve its usefulness and extend its longevity.

The house of God is built externally by evangelism, but it is also built internally by equipping the saints to grow and mature in their relationship with Jesus Christ.

The word "edifying" speaks of the church progressing from salvation to sanctification. It is a picture of the church doing more than just professing Jesus Christ and preaching Jesus Christ but also projecting Jesus.

Notice that Paul is not using the words "build up" to indicate an increase in the number of attendees on a given Sunday! Edification, or building up the body of Christ, is a major function in the work of the church. Much of the edification takes place in the public worship, but there are other areas as well such as Bible study classes, leadership training, workshops, conferences, etc.

The important issue here is not the quantity of saints but the quality of saints. Saints are equipped so that they can engage in edification of other saints! This is God's pattern for real "church growth"! The church, which is the body of Christ, is built up externally through evangelism (Matthew 28:19–20) as more believers are added, but the body is being built up internally through edification.

The disciple of Jesus Christ, in peace, look for ways to edify everyone we can. Romans 14:19 says, "Let us therefore, follow after the things with which make for peace, and things with which one may edify another." Paul used the word "us" which shows that these words are for every believer.

The phrase "follow after these things" means "to follow or press hard after or pursue with all your energy, like a runner in a race exerting with every fiber within him to reach the goal."

The word "peace" means to "join or bind together that which has been separated." Those who follow after Jesus Christ have been called to peace. Jesus said in Matthew 5:9, "Blessed are the peacemakers, for they will be called the sons of God." He didn't tell his followers to be "peacekeepers" but "peacemakers." This word *peacemakers* could be translated as "peace workers." To bring an end to conflict, it takes great effort. But we are doing what God does when we resolve conflict.

We will experience unity. "Until we all reach unity in the faith."

It is through the equipping of the saints that unity is attained in the body of Christ. Every Christian is involved, and every Christian is to be made ready to do the work. God himself initiated unity! Therefore, the unity in the church is a reflection of the unity that is found between the Father, Son, and Spirit. The reason Jesus wants unity in the church is so that other people will believe in him. When the church unity is introduced to the world, people will believe in Jesus Christ.

The word "reach" refers to travelers. Paul clearly implies that spiritual maturity is a process. He used the word "until" indicating that maturity will not be complete until Jesus Christ return to take us home to be with him, or until we die physically and go to be with him for eternity, arriving at their destination. Disunity often raises its ugly head when people sit on the sidelines and talk about their needs instead of serving in order to meet the needs of others.

The unity of the faith is the spiritual goal for the church to reach. The word "faith" in this verse is not referring to our belief at salvation, but it is referring to the Christian truth. When believers are properly taught and faithfully obeying Christ and allowing his Spirit to minister his gifts through them, then the result is the unity of the faith. The church of Corinth is a good example of how disunity occurs when believers are ignorant or disobedient of the Word of God.

We will have a renewed relationship with Christ. "And in the knowledge of the Son of God." Unity will produce the knowledge of the Son of God. The unity of the knowledge of the Son of God is defined by knowing who he is, what he has done, and what he has accomplished by the cross and his resurrection. It is by this unity that we are brought into completion and full maturity in Christ as his body. Not only will you know the Word of God, but you get to know the God of the Word.

The Greek word for "knowledge" in this verse is *epignosis* which means full knowledge—what is in your head begins to sink down into your heart. That is when a believer starts to grow, becoming what God wants us to be—to experience him, not just know about Him. You get to know him. The knowledge of the Son of God refers to an experiential knowledge gained by a daily walk with Christ. It is what Paul meant when he declared in Philippians 3:10, "That I may know him."

Some of us are like the little girl who had been trying for months to tie her own shoes. She finally figured it out, but then, she started crying. Her dad asked her why she was so sad, and she replied, "Because now I'll have to tie my shoes all by myself for the rest of my life." If we want to grow as a church, we must be involved in giving of our time, talents, and our treasures. We could say it like this: If you want to grow, then you must give what you've been given.

We will have a mature membership. "And become mature attaining to the whole measure of the fullness of Christ. Then we will no longer be infants." Paul, in writing about attaining the measure of the fullness of Christ, is saying that Jesus alone is to be our standard by which we measure our spiritual maturity.

Romans 8:29 says, "For those God foreknew he also predestined to be conformed to the likeness of his Son." God's goal for all of his children is that they would grow up and mature so that they can become like Christ.

We will experience spiritual stability. "Tossed back and forth by the waves, and blown here and there by every wind of teaching and by the cunning and craftiness of men in their deceitful scheming." To avoid being tossed back and forth and blown here and there by every wind of teaching is to hold unswervingly to the Word of God as the source of our beliefs. Believers should never consider anything as the truth until they have first tested it against the truth of the Word of God.

We will be linked in love. If we want to grow in love, then we must live lives serving. "Instead, speaking the truth in love, we will in all things grow up into him who is the Head, that is, Christ. A mark of maturity is speaking the truth in love, by doing this we will grow up in all aspects into Him, who is the head, even Christ." Love joined to truth is not simply concerned for feelings, but is concerned for God's best for the individual. Speaking the truth must be done in love or not done at all. So we must do it properly. It should never be done in haste. It should never be done while angry. It should never be done without much prayer and heart searching. We should never speak about someone to someone else. And it should always be done at the leading of the Lord. If done properly it can be redemptive.

Equipped with Spiritual Gifts

In preparing the believers to do the work of the ministry, leadership must help them to discover and exercise their spiritual gifts. When you become a Christian, God gives you at least one spiritual gift, and sometimes, more than one. You can't learn or earn spiritual gifts by any effort of your own; they are gifts from God. Every believer is a recipient of the gift or gifts from God and their benefits. When we are not functioning and exercising our *spiritual gifts*, we are actually "robbing" others of these needy benefits. The Bible tells us to desire them earnestly, to stir them up, and to encourage others.

In 1 Corinthians 12:1, the Apostle Paul writes, "Now concerning spiritual gifts, brethren, I would not have you ignorant." One of God's divine mandates is to dispel ignorance by feeding the flock with knowledge and understanding of the *spiritual.* According to Jeremiah 3:15, "And I will give you pastors according to my heart," says God, "which shall feed you with knowledge and understanding."

The reason so many believers are spiritually immature is because they have not been taught how they are to relate themselves to God spiritually and personally, and therefore, they not only misunderstand spiritual gifts, but they also misuse their spiritual gifts.

Bruce Bugbee, founder and president of Network Ministries, stated that "Spiritual gifts are divine abilities distributed by the Holy Spirit to every believer according to God's design and grace for the common good of the body of Christ."

Like children running to open their gifts on Christmas morning, followers of Jesus should have the same anticipation and excitement to unwrap their spiritual gifts. God is a gift-giving God. He does not give us gifts simply to secure our eternal relationship with him, but he gives us spiritual gifts so we can participate in what he is doing to redeem people to him.

There is no such thing as a believer without any gift who just comes to church. Peter tells us, "As each one has received a gift, minister it to one another" (1 Peter 4:10, NKJV). The phrase "each one" indicates that every Christian has at least one spiritual gift. In the phrase "minister it to one another," here the word minister means to serve. It is the same word from which we get "deacon." Deacon is a word that was commonly used for "table waiter." We should offer the gifts which God gives us to each other as a waiter offering a well-prepared meal to the guests—not with personal pride, because the waiter does not prepare the food; not keeping the food to ourselves, because it is not meant for us; but instead, enjoying the privilege of being the ones who "carry" God's grace from him to his people. One believer has the hors d'oeuvres. One carries a selection of the main courses. Another has the desserts. We are waiters! The food is given to a waiter or waitress so that they might distribute it to others. Just as spiritual gifts are given to us so that we might distribute them to others in the body.

Paul explains in 1 Corinthians 12:15–16 that a Christian cannot use his or her spiritual gift(s) effectively unless they exercise it in a local church. A believer with a spiritual gift but without a church is like a fish out of water.

Spiritual gifts are governed by design to be exercised within the church. A believer can come out of the church and exercise their gift for a limited period of time, but that gift will gradually die because it has been removed from the body of Christ. Your gift is to be used to help the body of Christ function in the world. For example, the spiritual gift of service is the hand of Christ in the world. People with this gift perform acts of service that demonstrate God's love to others. Another example is the gift of exhortation or encouragement that can be viewed as the arm of the church that you put around those who are discouraged or need someone to walk alongside them.

The first place in the New Testament where spiritual gifts are mentioned is in Romans 1:11. Paul says, "For I long to see you, that I may impart unto you some spiritual gift, to the end ye may be established." The words "impart to you some spiritual gift" can be translated "I long to see you that I may use my gifts to strengthen you." Therefore, it is clear from this text that spiritual gifts are for strengthening others.

To strengthen someone by a spiritual gift simply means to help that person to maintain their faith and not give up when they are facing trouble in their life. We use our spiritual gifts to help other people keep the faith.

Paul wanted to impart the spiritual blessings in order for the believers to be established. He wanted the brothers and sisters "to grow up in all aspects into Him, who is the head, even Christ" (Ephesians 4:15). If it doesn't benefit the body, it's not a gift.

Spiritual gifts are not natural talents or acquired skills. You can't learn or earn spiritual gifts by any effort of your own; they are gifts from God. A person may have a natural talent in some area but not be spiritually gifted in that area at all. Sometimes, talents and gifts go together, and sometimes, they don't.

Spiritual gifts are not the *fruit* of the Spirit. The fruit of the Spirit refers to the nine character qualities mentioned in Galatians 5:22–23 (love, joy, peace, patience, kindness, goodness, faithfulness, gentleness, self-control). All believers are to manifest these character qualities all the time, but they are not spiritual gifts.

Spiritual gifts are not for our own private benefit but for the common good. All of us are to use our unique spiritual gifts to serve God and others in specific ways both in the church and out in the world.

A spiritual gift is not a ministry role. That is, there is no such thing as the gift of youth work or the gift of writing Gospel music or the gift of men or women ministry or the gift of evangelizing Muslims. Those are area where believers use their gifts of teaching, evangelism, of service, and help in a particular way. But these gifts could be used in other ways as well.

Spiritual gifts are not for personal glory, personal influence, or personal gains. It says in 1 Peter 4:11, "That God in all things may be glorified through Jesus Christ, to whom be praise and dominion forever and ever. Amen." The word "that" in this verse tells us the final purpose for the use of spiritual gifts. We use our gifts so God might be glorified through Jesus Christ. This is the work of the Holy Spirit—to glorify God through Jesus Christ. God is not glorified unless you are serving in his strength. Therefore, the believer must take his or her eyes off self, schedule, abilities, desires, also their needs and comfort and serve for the glory of God. God gives us gifts, not to make us proud but to bring him glory, and that we may serve the body of Christ.

Steps to Equipping Others

The word "equip" is associated with the Word of God. Therefore, a disciple must be equipped from the Word of God. Paul says in 2 Timothy 3:16–17, "All Scripture is inspired by God and profitable for teaching, for reproof, for correction, for training in righteousness; that the man of God may be adequate, equipped for every good work."

The work of equipping the saints is to get them under the authority of God's Word. Equipping comes from the Word of God.

> Wherefore comfort yourselves together,
> and edify one another, even as also ye do.
> (1 Thessalonians 5:11)

The first step to EQUIP others is to *encourage* them.

To encourage someone means to "call to one's side." Making disciples must begin with having an intentional relationship in which you walk alongside other disciples, encouraging them, equipping them, and challenging them to grow in Christ.

You encourage someone when you stand alongside them for a period of time to comfort them and to assist them. In John 16:16–18, Jesus said to his disciples that he would send another Counselor to be with them forever. Another name for the Holy Spirit is "Encourager." Jesus said he would not leave his disciples as orphans. He would send his Holy Spirit to be with them. He equipped his followers by encouraging them to count on his power.

There are other words mentioned in the Bible that have similar meaning, such as exhort, warn, or admonish. People who encourage others say it with love what a person needs to hear, when they need to hear it, even if it isn't what the person wants to hear.

Encouragement is important because it helps us keep the faith. This world is opposed to the gospel. We need encouragement to continue standing firm for Christ in the midst of a world that rejects him. It also means that you're helping to develop something in the person.

We should never minister to others from a position of superiority, instead, encourage them as a fellow disciple, a fellow recipient of God's love and grace. Encouragement can come by sharing encouraging words or an understanding ear or a willingness to just listen. It can come in the form of a gift, a note, an act of service, or a word of appreciation. There are many ways in which we can encourage one another, but the main thing is to communicate that you love them and care about them.

> And the things that thou hast heard of me among many witnesses, the same commit thou to faithful men, who shall be able to teach others also. (2 Timothy 2:2)

The second step to EQUIP others is to *qualify* them. A leader qualifies those he leads by helping them to discover and know their skills and giftedness related to the ministry they are called to do. It has been said that "A good teacher is like a candle—it consumes itself to light the way for others."

The goal isn't just to give a person more head knowledge, but to give them the skills to follow Christ and to pass the faith on to others. So, equipping disciples is more than a Bible study or a Sunday school lesson. To disciple others requires the personal investment of Christ in you into the life of another. Paul tells us in 2 Timothy 2:2, "And the things that thou hast heard of me among many witnesses, the same commit thou to faithful men, who shall be able to teach others also."

In 2 Timothy 1:5, Paul warns Timothy about those men who wanted to be teachers but who had strayed from the goal of growing and maturing believers in the Lord. In verse 6, the word for "straying" in the Greek language is *astocheo*, which means "to fail to aim carefully, and thus to miss the mark." They were disqualified because they were aiming at the wrong goals.

> And it came to pass, that, as he was praying in a certain place, when he ceased, one of his disciples said unto him, Lord, teach us to pray, as John also taught his disciples. (Luke 11:1)

The third step to EQUIP others is to *understand* them. The leader must take time to watch them do ministry so that he/she can know and understand their needs and respond to them. One way to understand a person's need is to observe them in ministry. Another way to understand their need is to listen to them.

There were times the twelve disciples failed to understand; Jesus would patiently take them aside to review and explain (Matthew 13:36). He also taught one-on-one as when Mary sat at his feet to listen to him (Luke 10:39). Discipleship lessons need to be understood by the disciple if you expect healthy growth and maturity.

> These things command and teach. (1 Timothy 4:11)

The fourth step to EQUIP others is to *instruct* them. Instructing is part of leading. Followers need to know what is expected of them and how to do the task assigned to them. In Mark 10:44–45, Jesus instructed his disciples to have the attitude of a servant. In Luke 14:11, he taught them to humble themselves.

Jesus taught his disciples through an apprenticeship-style training. He did not set up a formal seminary but just spent time in the disciples' homes, walking with them, letting them observe his ministry, delegating responsibilities to his disciples, sending them out to preach, and having them report back to him.

To instruct others, prayer comes first. Pray for the person before giving a word of instruction to them. Pray to the Holy Spirit, asking him for guidance as to how to best approach the person, what to teach, and how to teach it. Also, search the Scriptures because it "is useful for teaching, for reproof, for correction, and for training in righteousness" (2 Timothy 3:16).

> I pray for them: I pray not for the world,
> but for them which thou hast given me; for they
> are thine. (John 17:9)

The fifth step to EQUIP other is to *pray* for them. The power of equipping others is not in technique but in prayer. Prayer gives discernment, protection, and power to those who lead. Prayer is God's answer to our weakness as leaders. Jesus prayed for his disciples' ministry. He prayed that they would remain one in purpose (John 17:11). He prayed that they would have joy in their ministry (John 17:13). He prayed for their protection from the evil one (John 17:15), and he prayed that they be made holy by the word of God (John 17:17).

A mentor not only imparts wisdom to the person they are mentoring, but they also become that person's number one prayer warrior. A mentor should have at the top of their prayer list the name of their mentored and should know exactly how to pray for them because of their kindred relationship.

We must pray for the spiritual growth of the new believers, trusting God to work in their lives. Praying with them shows that we care for them. It also gives them an example of what it looks like to communicate with God the Father.

Apart from our prayers and the prayers of others, no growth will take place. We must rely on God to accomplish this work in a believer's life. Pray for others, and pray for yourself.

The Marks of Spiritual Growth in the Disciple

Growth is a condition of discipleship. If a disciple is a learner, then growth is implied in the very definition of the word. Growth is expected of every disciple of Jesus Christ. When a person has been a Christian for many years and still has not grown or developed beyond those opening stages, then something is wrong.

Some years ago, soft drink bottles had a slogan inscribed on them that said, "No deposit, No return." This is true of every Christian; many are not getting any return because they are not making any deposit. There are some things that a Christian can do to help himself or herself to grow.

The first mark of an equipped disciple is faithfulness (John 8:31–32). Jesus said, "If you continue in my word, then you are my disciples indeed" (John 8:31). A disciple is one who, on a daily basis, continues in the Word of God. We cannot grow as Christians without studying the Bible.

Peter described the Word of God as milk (1 Peter 2:1–2). Just as newborn babies need milk to grow, a new believer need the Word of God to grow to spiritual maturity.

If anyone is going to be a disciple, then he or she must get a grip on the milk bottle and keep feeding on the Word of God. A disciple must get a grip because one of Satan's tactics is to snatch the Word of God away from the believer to keep them from growing into a mature disciple. There are several ways to grip the Word of God:

- *We must receive the word.* This is where discipleship begins. We receive the Word by hearing the Word which brings about faith (Romans 10:17). Receiving the Word is the equivalent to receiving the Lord Jesus Christ. Jesus is the incarnate Word (John 1:1–5, 14). To reject the Word is to reject the Lord.
- *We must meditate upon the word.* To continue in Christ's Word is not automatic; it is the result of strong purpose and self-discipline. Therefore, we must "study" and be "a workman" (2 Timothy 2:15). We should read it daily and carefully observing what is being said to us. Psalm 1:2 tells us that the man who is blessed is one who meditates on God's Law day and night. This principle goes back to the Old Testament where Moses told the Israelites to write the Law on the gates and doorposts and to bind them to their wrists (Deuteronomy 11:18).
- *We must study, persevere, and continue to understand and comprehend God's word.* "The disciple also studies the Scriptures for the purpose of learning the mind of Christ."

Every Christian must have a regular time to study God's Word. It may be systematically reading the Bible, or it may be a topical study of various subjects in the Bible. It may be following a simple guide to Bible study. No matter what method is used, it is important that every Christian study God's Word.

James tells us that we must be doers of the Word and not just hearers (James 1:22). This is the essence of "continue in"—to make it their rule of life in daily practice. At times, the teachings are hard to understand or to practice. This can be seen in John 6:66: when Jesus's teaching about flesh and blood occurred, many disciples left him. However, a true disciple continued to abide in the Word of Jesus even when it was difficult to understand or difficult to obey.

The second mark of an equipped disciple is fruitfulness (John 15:2–8).

Our job is not producing fruit. Our job is to abide or remain in Christ, and if we do, the Holy Spirit will produce the fruit, and this fruit is the result of our obedience. As we become more obedient to the Lord and learn to walk in his ways, our lives will change. The biggest change will take place in our hearts, and the overflow of this will be new conduct (thoughts, words, and actions) representative of that change. The change we seek is done from the inside out, through the power of the Holy Spirit. It isn't something we can conjure up on our own.

In verse 2, Jesus uses the phrase "in me." He is telling us that he is speaking here to people who are in a life-giving relationship to himself; he is speaking to those who are saved. No one can be considered a branch in the Lord's *vine* unless there is a vital connection to him. No one can bear fruit for the glory of the Lord unless they are attached to the *vine*. There are six times in these verses Jesus uses the phrase "in me."

How does a person abide in Jesus? First, you must be "in" Jesus. You must be saved! After that, you abide in him through prayer, study and meditate upon his Word, worship and praise him, and totally surrender your life to him.

Notice in these verses that the Lord expects us to bear fruit. There is to be a progression in our fruit bearing. He mentions "no fruit," "fruit," "more fruit," and "much fruit." This indicates that God expects us to always be growing in the fruit-bearing process.

What exactly will be produced in our lives when we do bear fruit? There are some basic fruits the Lord bears in the lives of his children. They are:

- The *fruit* in our life which is the *fruit* of the Spirit (Galatians 5:22–23).
- The *fruit* of our lips which is our praise and worship to him (Hebrews 13:15).
- The *fruit* of our labor which is the fruit of our walk; we behave more like him (Matthew 5:16).

- The *fruit* of love, which is our *witness* to others; we're burdened like Him (Matthew 9:36–38).

The quality of that fruit is not our responsibility. We are simply to abide. He will bring the kind of fruit through us that pleases him. The quantity of that fruit is not our responsibility. Our duty as his disciples is to abide in him. He will produce the quality and the quantity of fruit from our lives that pleases him. If we could ever fully understand the truth that being a fruitful Christian is about abiding, it would make a world of difference in our lives.

John 15:6 tells us that not every branch responds properly to the pruning or cleansing ministry of the *gardener*. When this happens, there is a loss of fellowship and of reward. Here is what Jesus is talking about:

- Fellowship is lost; cast out—*not abiding* (This is not about your salvation; it is about your fellowship). There is a relationship that won't be denied! The branch still possesses the same nature as the Vine, but it is no longer attached in the sense of life-drawing fellowship.
- Vitality is lost; withered—possessing no life, or dead and dried up. This describes many Christians today! There is deadness where there used to be life. There is weakness where there used to be power. There is emptiness where there used to be fullness. The idea is to come back and renew that lost fellowship. Our connection to him in fellowship allows us to draw the life-giving juice from the *vine* and will begin to produce fruit in us for him.
- Reward is lost. When this life is over, there will be many who are called by the name of Jesus but were unfruitful. They will experience the loss of reward (1 Corinthians 3:13–15). Many think they will be content just to get to Heaven, but there should be a desire to have rewards to place at his feet. Will you hear, "Well done?" Only if you are a fruitful branch!

One part of the mission of a disciple is that he or she is called to bear fruit. In John 15:16, Jesus said, "Ye have not chosen me, but I have chosen you, and ordained you, that ye should go and bring forth fruit, and that your fruit should remain; that whatever ye shall ask of the father in my name, he may give it you." To live as a fruit-bearing disciple of Jesus Christ is an appointment from God the Father. The word appointed means "to put in place" or "I have set you in me."

If Jesus Christ does the choosing, obedience to his commands isn't initiated by the disciples but by him because he has said in John 15:5, "Without me ye can do nothing." This means we place our confidence in the vine to give us everything necessary to bear fruit!

Jesus said, if we remain in him, we're going to receive what he has for us. The fruit doesn't just come and go according to how we are feeling or how we are doing that week; but the fruit is the work of Jesus Christ according to his choosing! What he begins, he will also end, and this is our confidence in asking anything of the Father. If he gave us Jesus Christ, and if he's pleased with Jesus Christ, then we trust he's pleased with us too, and he will give us whatever we need to walk like him and glorify his name. When we witness to others and win them to Jesus Christ, this is bringing forth fruit to the glory of God the father.

The third mark of an equipped disciple is fellowship (John 13:34–35).

The word "fellowship" is translated from the Greek word *koinonia* which means, "sharing in common." It is one of the ways we express love and respect for one another. This is the kind of love Jesus commands of those who follow him. He said, "By this all men will know" that we are truly his disciples.

The Old Testament taught people to "love your neighbor as yourself" (Leviticus 19:18). But Jesus said in John 13:34–35, "A new commandment I give unto you, that ye love one another; as I have loved you, that ye also love one another".

Therefore, fellowship is love for other disciples. We are also told that love of other believers is the evidence of our being a member of God's family (1 John 3:10).

Love is defined in 1 Corinthians 13:1–13. These verses show us that love is not an emotion; it is action. Furthermore, we are told to think more highly of others than of ourselves and to look out for their interests (Philippians 2:3–4).

Fellowship builds faith. The importance of fellowship with our brothers and sisters is that it helps to build our faith. We cannot stay strong in our faith without contact with our brothers and sisters in Christ. When God's children spend time talking about the Lord with other brothers and sisters in Christ, their faith is built up.

Christianity is a unique religion in that it is not a completely individualized religion. In Christianity, we lean on other people called by the same name to help us to grow and to mature in our individual faith.

Fellowship builds accountability. One reason to show such love is because this is not simply a command to love one another but a command to love one another in a special way. Jesus is calling us to a higher standard of love!

Why we should be devoted to fellowshipping is because it builds accountability. Another Christian outside of your immediate family can talk to you about things that you are struggling with in your faith and help to check up on you and to encourage you.

Fellowship builds unity! It is said that there can be union without unity. Just tie two cats' tails together and throw them over a clothes-line. The church is called to be united. Many times in the church there is union; we meet together, but this is not unity. Unity is every-thing in common and being of the same mind. This does not mean that we will not disagree, but this just means we will disagree in love.

The church is called the family of God, and we as the church are all one body, and each member is important. That is why it hurts the whole body when someone skips church. When someone misses church, it is as if a part of the body is not present. We cannot be fully functional as the church if members of the body are not worshipping with the rest of the body.

Fellowship builds relationships! To build good friendships in the church, you need to get involved with things in the church. You cannot expect good relationships to be built if you are not fellowshipping with other Christians. If Jesus Christ is at the center, then marriages are stronger and friendships are stronger. Fellowship builds relationships mainly because of the encouragement that is received from brothers and sisters when fellowshipping with one another.

Fellowship keeps brothers and sisters from sin (Hebrews 3:13). The fellowship that we have with each other is extremely important to individual spiritual well-being. We are obligated to fellowship regularly so we can encourage each other and help each other from falling into sin.

Assembling together is essential. It is very important to have Christian friends rather than non-Christian friends, but choose your friends wisely. The Word of God makes it clear that we are to meet together formally and corporately as the body of Christ (Hebrews 10:25). If you want to grow in your faith, then you must come to church. The fellowship that we gain from studying of the Scriptures together and praying together builds our faith. The Scriptures give a command for us not to forsake assembling together.

Fellowship builds the kingdom. Another great benefit of fellowship between Christians is that it builds the kingdom. Because of the fellowship that Christians enjoy, more souls are brought to Jesus (Acts 2:47).

It builds the *local body*! When Christians regularly meet together to fellowship, people in the community will be drawn into that fellowship, and that local body will grow and will increase.

Our fellowship is a witness to the community. We have to do whatever it takes to spend more time with one another in and out of church; this is a great witness to the community. When people see such a close-knit group of people, they will want to be a part of the fellowship there.

This is important to the kingdom. Not simply because we want a few more number on our attendance, but because the body is not complete without one person. When the community sees a member of the church not devoted to fellowship, they will assume there is nothing different about those friendships and relationships than any other relationships.

Equipped for Spiritual Warfare

There is real spiritual warfare being waged by Satan and his demons against God and his people. See Ephesians 6:10–18—Satan versus God. Spiritual warfare is also a real power struggle with the ways of the world versus God's ways. The world lures us. It's not neutral. Paul pleads to all believers in Romans 12:1–2, "I beseech you therefore, brethren, by the mercies of God, that ye present your bodies a living sacrifice, holy, acceptable unto God, which is your reasonable service. And be not conformed to this world: but be ye transformed by the renewing of your mind that ye may prove what is that good, and acceptable, and perfect will of God."

Tony Evans said in his message on *spiritual warfare*, "Surrounding us is a spiritual war, angels versus demons; good versus evil and light versus darkness. But amazingly, most believers live as if this conflict were not even happening, as if the "battle of the ages" was just a fantasy or sci-fi story. Yet not one of us is immune to the consequences of spiritual warfare. Although the players fight in an invisible realm, we all face the effects—pain, struggle, defeat, heartache—of their conflict every day of our lives."

The devil's primary strategy is to disguise his activities so that it appears that someone or something else is to blame. He wants us to get our attention off of his surrogates, his instruments, his hindrances and not "wrestle" with them so that our battle will be directed against the "symptoms" instead of the "real source." We all know that a decongestant will help relieve a stuffy nose, but it will not cure a cold. Likewise, you can fight with the symptoms of the

Devil, but you will not end the problems until you deal with the source and bind the "strong man."

Remember when Peter resisted Jesus's decision to return to Jerusalem, knowing that he would be crucified there? Jesus did not rebuke Peter, but turned to Peter and rebuked Satan. "Get behind me Satan" (Matthew 16:23). Peter wasn't demon possessed and probably didn't intend to be an offense, however, the Devil inspired Peter's statement, and Jesus went after the real source.

Paul said that our battle is not with "flesh and blood, but against principalities" (Ephesians 6:12). How important it is that we understand what the real root of the problem is and who our real enemy is. It is Satan—not flesh and blood, not our brethren, not our family, not our children, not husbands and wives, not employers, nor our government! The Devil is the enemy!

One day, after Jesus had cast out a demon and healed a deaf and mute boy, Jesus explained that in order to overturn the works and activities of the Devil, we must bind him first. Jesus said, "Or else how can one enter into a strong man's house, and spoil his goods, except he first bind the strong man? And then he will spoil his house" (Matthew 12:29). In order to neutralize the Devil's works, we must go and deal directly with the source and bind up the devil so that his hands are tied. Often, the local churches suffer senseless conflicts or unexplained problems. The congregations experience little growth, and the preaching of the Word is not easily proclaimed or well received by the community. Understand this, behind the scene, Satan is the culprit.

Satan uses a wide variety of tactics to lure God's people into sin and disqualify them from ministry and being effective in the Kingdom of God. There are four basic tactics that he uses to harm God's people and the Kingdom of God:

- *Temptation*. Matthew 4:3–4 states, "The tempter came to him and said, If you are the Son of God, tell these stones to become bread. Jesus answered, "It is written: 'Man does not live on bread alone, but on every word that comes from the mouth of God.'" Temptation is to sow the seeds of doubt that God's way is not the best way for us to live. Satan is the one behind the temptations of mankind. Scripture is full of examples of this strategy such as Eve in the Garden of Eden, Judas the disciple who betrayed Jesus, and Jesus himself in the wilderness.

Believers do not have the power to resist the devil on their own. Although God allows Satan to tempt Christians, he always provides them with a way out. It says in 1 Corinthians 10:13, "No temptation has overtaken you except such as is common to man; but God is faithful, who will not allow you to be tempted beyond what you are able, but with the temptation will also make the way of escape, that you may be able to bear it."

- *Accusation.* In Revelation 12:10, Satan is called "the *accuser* of the brethren." He seeks to keep us in conflict with the world and with one another, and he tries to get us to question our standing before God. Satan will often bring accusations to a person against God. He whispers in the ear of the unbelievers, "Don't ever become a Christian! You will really ruin your life!" If you are a believer, he says, "God doesn't even exist. God doesn't care about you or your life."

  Satan causes the unbelievers to accuse us of acts that are unbecoming of a Christian. He incites division among believers so they will accuse each other. Satan loves to tear apart the local church from within. He also uses our sins against us by continually telling us we are not good enough to be a Christian.

Deception. It tells us in 2 Corinthians 11:14 that Satan disguises himself as an angel of light. He seeks to blind us to the truth and deceive us into thinking counterfeits are the real thing. He tells us lies about God, the world, and ourselves, hoping we will believe them. He offers false teachers, promises, peace, joy, and happiness as a way to keep us from the biblical truth.

Direct attacks. Satan seeks to attack us directly through demonic activity, human agents, or institutions. He causes demons to attack and oppress. He uses humans to persecute. He uses institutions, such as government, to hinder the growth of Christianity.

Every Christian must be aware that God has equipped them to overcome Satan's power. The Apostle Paul said that, "For the weapons of our warfare are not carnal, but mighty through God to the pulling down of strong holds" (2 Corinthians 10:4).

Many times, God's people are guilty of fighting the wrong foe! We get at odds with our fellow believers when the real enemy is the devil! He is a master at sowing discord among the brethren. We need to remember that our fight is a spiritual battle.

The devil might work through people at times to get to us and cause us to stumble, but the real battle is fought on a spiritual level. Our battle is with an unseen army of spiritual enemies led by the devil himself. Since our enemy is a spiritual enemy, some people might wonder how we go about knowing how to fight him. We need to learn from God's Word that teach us how to be more than conquerors in Jesus Christ.

Ephesians 6:11 tells us, "Put on the whole armor of God, that you may be able to stand against the wiles of the devil." The armor is of God. It is not armor that man has devised or constructed. It is armor that has been constructed by God. You must put the armor on yourself; God will not put it on for you. Every disciple should be taught how to put on the armor of God.

The phrase "put on" carries the idea of doing something once and for all. It speaks of permanence. The full armor of God is not something the disciple put on and then take off again, but we are to keep it on at all times.

The equipment that God gives his people starts with the *belt* of truth. The Greek word for "truth" in this passage is a peculiar word. The word "truth" (*alethia*) refers to something that has been "laid tangibly and clearly before our eyes."

It is a weapon that we can (1) see with our eyes, (2) hold with our hands, and (3) read with our mouths, (4) hide in our hearts, (5) keep as our possession.

The first piece of armor is the *belt of truth*. The belt is known as the cingulum or *balteus*; it played a crucial role in the effectiveness of a soldier's armor. It was the belt that held the scabbard or sash, without which, there would be no place to put a sword. Imagine a soldier, fired up and charging out into battle without his belt and, consequently, without his weapon!

In addition, "strips of leather hung from the belt to protect the lower body." Some commentaries say the belt "girds on [secures] all the other pieces of our armor." Therefore, truth should cleave to us like a belt cleaves to our body.

It holds the breastplate in place. If the breastplate sagged, then vital organs like the heart and lungs are exposed. It had a clip on it, on which the shield rested, so the arms of the soldier did not get weary.

The belt of truth is followed by the encouragement to put on the *breastplate of righteousness*. Because the Word of Truth has defined for us that which is right and that which is wrong, one of the most important jobs of the breastplate is to protect the heart. Biblically, the word heart means the inner part of the mind—the inner being of a man. What is in our heart determines what we are. As Proverbs 4:23 tells us, "Above all else guard your heart; for out of it are the issues of life."

To put on the breastplate of righteousness is to dedicate yourself to a life of self-control. Like a soldier who accepts the weight and constraints of bulky and heavy armor, the disciple of Christ consents to live within the boundaries of self-denial and submission to God's standard of righteousness. The soldiers of God in this world do so to protect themselves from the outward dangers of battle. The Christian does so protect himself from himself.

The *preparation of the Gospel of peace* is the next piece of the Christian's armor that must be worn at all times. The English Standard version of this passage says, "And, as shoes for your feet, having put on the readiness given by the gospel of peace." A good pair of shoes allows the soldier to be ready for conflict. In the same way, we are to be prepared for spiritual battle by having our shoes on—the shoes of the gospel of peace. The word preparation refers to being in the condition of readiness or preparedness.

It is called the gospel of "peace" because it is the peace brought to us by the gospel that provides us protection. The "preparation" of the gospel of peace speaks of those who are ready to move, those who are ready to take the gospel wherever God leads them. The shoes of the Gospel of peace help us to remember to follow Jesus. When we are following Jesus and doing what he wants us to do, we cannot follow Satan, and we cannot do what Satan wants us to do. It is important to put on the shoes of the Gospel of peace every day so we can tell others about Jesus and keep ourselves from following Satan.

This Gospel of peace is seen three ways in the believer's life. First, there is peace with God. This type of peace comes from receiving Christ as Lord and Savior (Romans 5:1). Second, there is peace with one another. Every believer should take the lead in seeing there is peace in the family. Each believer should do his or her part to ensure there will be no place for trouble and disunity in God's house (Hebrews 12:14; Romans 12:18). Third, there is the peace of God. The peace of God means that you do not allow the *chaos* to control you. This type of peace comes by trusting in Christ (Isaiah 29:3; John 14:1–2).

The fourth piece of armor is the *shield of faith*.

The Bible says "the shield of faith" will enable us to "quench all the fiery darts of the wicked." In the days of the Roman Empire, the tips of arrows would be wrapped in pieces of cloth that had been soaked in pitch. This would then be set on fire and shot at the enemy. When the arrow hit its target, the flaming pitch would splatter in every direction, igniting everything flammable it touched. The arrows could cause damage by piercing bodies. The pitch could cause serious burns in their skin, and it could burn their equipment and gear.

The Roman shield would provide an adequate defense against the fiery darts. If the shield was metal, the arrow and its fiery tip would be deflected. If the shield was leather, it would be soaked in water prior to the battle, and the wet leather would quench the fiery arrows and protect the soldier behind the shield.

Every day, the saints of God are under attack by the "fiery darts" of the devil. The arrows he launches against us are usually the arrows of temptation. Satan attacks us with temptations of sexual immorality, hatred, envy, anger, covetousness, envy, fear, despair, distrust, doubt, pride, and every other conceivable sin. The "fiery darts" of temptation can bring great damage to our lives, but the "shield of faith" has the power to quench all the devil's fiery darts!

The *faith* that Paul refers to here is not the doctrines we believe. He is referring to simple childlike faith in Jesus Christ—simple trust in what he says in his Word. Trust him to love you, provide for you and protect you. Trust him to make "all things work together for good to those who love the Lord and are called according to his purpose" (Romans 8:28).

The fifth piece of armor is the *helmet of salvation*. Ephesians 6:17 says that the spiritual "helmet" we are to wear in our spiritual battles is the "helmet of salvation." The helmet was used to protect against blows to the head. This indicates that Satan's blows are aimed at our minds, i.e., the thoughts. The vital part of our victory lies in our ability to think right. His intent is to destroy our sense of security and our assurance in Jesus Christ. If Satan can strike a blow against us that causes us to become discouraged and filled with doubt, he will have little trouble sidelining us and taking us out of the battle.

The helmet also protected the eyes of the soldier, enabling him to maintain physical vision. Spiritual vision allows the Christian to fix his or her eyes on the goal, pressing forward without distraction or detours.

In Ephesians 6:17, Paul uses the word "take" which literally means, receive, accept, or welcome. When Paul says "take the helmet of salvation," he is not referring to being saved. He is speaking to people who are already saved. What he means here is that we are to *stand* in the full assurance of the salvation we possess in the Lord Jesus Christ. When Satan comes against you, take your stand with your "helmet of salvation" on, knowing that you belong to the Lord Jesus Christ.

The final piece of that armor is the *sword of the Spirit*, which is the word of God.

The short sword that was carried by every Roman foot soldier was the principal weapon he used in hand to hand combat. It was carried in a scabbard, attached to the soldier's belt, so that it was always available and ready for use. The Spirit of God has given the Christian a powerful weapon which is the Word of God.

Like any tool or weapon, the Bible is not much good to us if we are not skilled in its use. In the hands of a skilled swordsman, a sword is a deadly, powerful weapon. In the hands of a novice, there is a real danger of harming oneself as much as harming the enemy. The disciple must put time and effort into learning to use the Word of God.

In Ephesians 6:17, the Apostle Paul is not referring to the entire Bible, as such. In the Greek language, the translation for "word" is not *logos* but *rhema*. The word *rhema* literally means "an utterance." *Rhema* refers to a specific portion of the Scriptures that pertains to a specific subject or applies to a specific situation. It is a particular passage of scripture that is relevant to the particular need at hand.

The best example that we have of the use of Scripture to beat back temptation is the occasion of Satan's attack on Jesus, recorded in Matthew 4:1–11. Every time Satan tempted Jesus to get him to satisfy his fleshly desires, fleshly pride, and fleshly ego, Jesus countered the temptation with "It is written." Jesus was so familiar with the Word of God that he was able to select the proper *rhema* in each attack. His wise use of the *rhema* in the *logos* allowed him to achieve victory over the devil.

This indicates that the Bible is a defensive weapon, but it is also an offensive weapon. It allows us to take the battle to the enemy. Hebrews 4:12 says, "For the word of God is quick, and powerful, and sharper than any two-edged sword, piercing even to the dividing asunder of soul and spirit, and the intents of the heart."

The fourth piece of armor is prayer. According to James 4:7, when the Word of God is used against the devil, he will flee. Paul doesn't compare any of the other weapon to this last weapon because none of them come even close to the power and precision and effectiveness of this last weapon. As we wear the armor of God for battle, Paul tells us in Ephesians 6:18, "Praying always with all prayer and supplication in the Spirit, and watching thereunto with all perseverance and supplication for all saints." The phrase is, literally, "at every opportunity." It's the same idea as 1 Thessalonians 5:17, "Pray without ceasing." When you pray without ceasing, you will see things from God's viewpoint and not your own.

To pray without ceasing means you are depending on God in every area of your life. The Greek word translated *without ceasing* was used of a hacking cough and of repeated military assaults. Someone with a hacking cough does not cough every second, but rather, he coughs repeatedly and often. He never goes very long without coughing.

So it is in a military attack; the army makes an attack then regroups and attacks again and attacks again until it conquers the objective. That's the way that we should pray—repeatedly, over and over again until we gain the thing for which we are praying.

Paul uses the word "watching" in this verse. It is the same as to *be alert*; it also ties in with the analogy of the military. Like a soldier on guard duty. You have to watch, be alert for any signs of the enemy trying to attack, and when you see him, you go immediately to prayer.

Jesus said in Luke 18:1, "Men must always pray and not faint."

Equipped to Be Good Stewards

The word stewardship comes from the Greek word *oikenomous*, which means somebody who manages a household. A person doesn't own the household but manages it. In short, a steward is one who manages the possessions of another.

God owns everything. Everything means everything. "The earth is the Lord's and the fullness thereof, the world, and they that dwell therein" (Psalm 24:1). This is the fundamental principle of biblical stewardship. God owns everything; we are simply stewards, managers, or administrators acting on his behalf. We are not the owners, but we have been entrusted with resources and the care of everything—from our physical bodies, families, gifts, talents, money, time, and the gospel—for the sake of God's purposes in the world. The Bible makes it clear that God created everything, and even though he has entrusted much to each of us, his name is still on the title as the owner, and we are his stewards.

Every disciple must be equipped to practice good stewardship. A disciple is a good steward who knows and understands that everything in life is a gift freely given to us by the Lord, both to enrich us and also to bless and benefit others. Therefore, stewardship is responsibility with accountability. Stewardship is more than how we manage our finances and our faithfulness in paying God's tithes and offerings. In fact, it's more than just the management of our time, our possessions, our environment, or our health. Stewardship is our obedient witness to God's sovereignty. It's what motivates the followers of Christ to move into action, doing deeds that shows their belief in Christ. Paul's stewardship involved proclaiming that which Christ entrusted to him—the gospel (Ephesians 3:1–3). Every one of us is responsible for what has been given to us by God's revelation from Scripture, and we are going to be held responsible for what we've done with the knowledge of God's amazing grace.

As stewards of God, we are managers of that which belongs to God, and we are under his authority as we administer his affairs. As a disciple of Christ, good and faithful stewardship means that we fully acknowledge we are not our own but belong to Christ, the Lord, who gave himself for us. True stewardship is not about what we do but rather, about who we are and whose we are. It defines a way of life for every disciple.

Stewardship demands a commitment to others. It is our response to God's goodness to us. Stewardship is not doing something for God with your money, but doing something for others with his money. You act on God's behalf and in his name. Paul described himself as a slave to everyone (1 Corinthians 9:19) and always seeking the good of them (1 Corinthians 10:24, 33). Stewardship is both an expression of your love for God and the realization of that love in your relationships to others.

Biblical stewardship calls a Christian to give back to God through tithes and offerings. A disciple, therefore, must be taught to set aside a portion of his or her income for God. God wants you give to him to reflect your faith in him. When we acknowledge that we are God's stewards, and that he will meet our true needs, we demonstrate that faith by giving back to him in obedience to him. It takes faith to trust that God will meet our needs when we offer some of it back to him. It's much like a farmer who must reserve some of the crop to use as seed for another year. If he were to eat all of the harvest, he would soon become destitute. Instead, he must exercise faith that God will continue to provide by planting some of the seed into the ground. We reap what we sow. In 2 Corinthians 9:6–7, it says, "Now this I say, he who sows sparingly will also reap sparingly, and he who sows bountifully will also reap bountifully. Each one must do just as he has purposed in his heart, not grudgingly or under compulsion, for God loves a cheerful giver."

In Matthew 25:14–30, we see the master entrusting different amounts of his wealth to his "stewards" to manage just before leaving on a long journey. This passage points out some important characteristics of the role of a steward and his relationship with the master.

The master determined the amount each steward was to manage. The steward did not control the amount to be managed, only the decisions regarding its usage.

The master expected each steward to be faithful with his wealth. A steward who is unwise in managing the master's money loses the right be called a steward.

Even though it may take a while, there will eventually be a time when each steward is called to account by the master for his stewardship. A steward will be asked the question, "What did you do with what I gave you?"

The amount gained was not the issue but the faithfulness displayed. The master gave the same hearty, "Well done, my good a faithful servant (steward)" to the one who doubled his five bags of gold as the one who gained only two.

Observing faithfulness in his stewards brought happiness to the master. The master's reaction shows not only his joy but a desire to share an even closer relationship with his stewards.

The unfaithful steward failed in his role as steward driven by fear. "I was afraid and went and hid thy talent in the earth." His fear was so great it clouded his thinking. He did not even consider leaving it with the bankers to at least gain some interest.

There are negative ramifications to unfaithfulness by a steward. Not only is the trust relationship with the master damaged, but his unfaithfulness disqualified him from being a steward in the future. The gold he failed to steward wisely was given to another who had proven himself to be trustworthy.

Every believer has been called to be a good steward of God resources. We must take that role seriously as we seek someday to hear our Heavenly Father say, "Well done, my good a faithful servant (steward)!"

PART 3

Evangelizing the Sinner

And Jesus came and spake unto them, saying, all power is given unto me in heaven and in earth. Go ye therefore, and teach all nations, baptizing them in the name of the Father, and of the Son, and of the Holy Ghost: Teaching them to observe all things whatsoever I have commanded you: and, lo, I am with you always, even unto the end of the world. Amen. (Matthew 28:18–20, KJV)

Evangelizing the Sinner through Witnessing

Evangelism is the heart of our Christian faith, and we must train new believers how to be a witness for the Lord. We must teach them that every Christian must evangelize. Evangelism is not always experienced as good news simply because the believer does not know how to effectively share their faith. No ministry in the church is more vital than *evangelism*. It involves telling the good news, announcing the kingdom of God, and bearing witness. Evangelism is God's activity from beginning to end, for the carrying out under his authority, by his power, to fulfill a purpose which he determined before the creation of the world.

One of the most common misunderstandings in our day is that man somehow cooperates with God in bringing about salvation. People believe that they must be good to be accepted. Or that they must do certain things to please the Lord and earn his good favor. However, nothing could be farther from the truth! Salvation is the work of God. God's purpose for every believer is to make us the instrument for carrying out of his eternal purpose of salvation to the lost.

Evangelism begins and continues on in discipleship. God has given every generation of believers the responsibility and privilege of serving his purpose in the world. In 1 Timothy 2:2, the Apostle Paul helps us to understand that the growing, maturing Christian is one who is committed to leading another person to Christ and to nurture that person so they, too, can also lead others to Christ. This is the way in which evangelism is a part of the discipleship process. Disciples evangelize in order to disciple.

Evangelizing the sinner requires our time and faith. Going out to reach others for Christ with the gospel will take time. The disciple who wants to be about the business of evangelism must set aside time to reach that goal. That means rethinking our activities and rearranging our priorities to make time to do so.

The Apostle Paul felt indebted to Jesus Christ who had sacrifice himself to pay for Paul's sins and set him free from judgment and death. Paul said in Romans 1:14, "I am a debtor both to Greeks and to Barbarians, both to wise and to unwise." This sense of indebtedness to Christ made Paul a debtor to everyone who needed Jesus Christ the Savior.

Every servant of Jesus Christ who has received the truth has received it as a steward and, as such, is indebted both to God from whom he received it and to mankind for whom he received it. For the Gospel was given to us for others.

Defining Evangelism

Evangelism is teaching, proclaiming, or preaching the gospel—the message from God that leads us to salvation. The aim (hope, desire, goal) is to persuade (convince, convert). Evangelism is a term used in referring to the preaching of the Gospel. It comes from the same Greek word for gospel (*euangelizo*) and means "to bring or announce good news." Therefore, when we evangelize, we are spreading the "good news" of Jesus Christ to the lost. One of the clearest verses on evangelism is Philemon 1:6, "That the communication of thy faith may become effectual by the acknowledging of every good thing which is in you in Christ Jesus."

Jesus Christ gives an explicit commission to his followers to "Go into all the world and preach the gospel to every creature" (Mark 16:15). The Great Commission is not an option, it is not negotiable, it is not adjustable to our plans, but it is our supreme obligation. It is, "Whatever the Lord commands, that we will do." It must become evident to us, that the life and death and resurrection of Christ should affect our speech, conduct, and work.

The Apostle Paul, in his letter to the Romans, indicated that he was not ashamed of the Gospel (Romans 1:16). Many believers get ashamed and close their mouths when they sense that it is socially unacceptable to speak of the Gospel, and some are afraid that it sounds too simple.

The word "ashamed" means "disgraced" or "personally humiliated." A person "ashamed" in this way is like someone singled out for misplacing his or her trust in something, and that something let him or her down.

So when Paul says that he is not ashamed of the Gospel, he is saying his confidence in the Gospel is not misplaced. There is no disgrace in declaring it. Paul was not ashamed of the Gospel of Christ because he felt it to be the power of God to the salvation of all unbelievers, both Jews and Gentiles. To live and not be ashamed of the gospel means that we allow it to dominate our lives to the extent that everyone can see that we have "been with Jesus"

As part of the Great Commission found in Matthew 28:19–20, evangelism is one way in which we can fulfill Christ's call to be his witnesses (Acts 1:8). It is simply sharing the Word of God with others.

The Gospel, which is the Word of God, is what transforms the hearts of people. It's the truth that sets us free. No other message on planet earth transforms people into saints. Peter's sermon on the day of Pentecost was full of God's Word. He pointed to what God was doing in those days and showed how God had prophesied about that unique moment in his Word. As God formed the church out of the three thousand saved at Pentecost, the church was devoted to the apostles' teaching.

The definition of *evangelism* is the spreading of God's true plan of salvation, known as the Gospel, to non-Christians through words and deeds. Evangelism is a critical part of the Christian's life because Jesus Christ commanded us to spread the Gospel.

The Great Commission is the reason for our salvation. We are not saved by a church or by a preacher or by a doctrine or by a ritual. We are saved by a person, a living person who commissioned people to bring the Gospel to us.

Missions are the whole program, the plan; evangelism is the main means to fulfill the mission that our Lord gave to us to finish. Worship includes announcing him to a lost world and declaring his glory to all the people. This is a daily witnessing that involves speaking highly of God to others. It's telling your friends, your family, and your community about the "good news" that Jesus saves.

When you fall in love with the Lord Jesus Christ, you want to tell everyone you know. That's why Paul said in Romans 1:16, "For I am not ashamed of the Gospel of Christ; for it is the power of God unto salvation to everyone that believes; to the Jew first, and also to the Greek."

He was willing to preach it, because unless people hear the Gospel, they have no opportunity to believe and receive its salvation. The believer must not be ashamed to share the Gospel of Jesus Christ. Romans 10:11 tells says, "For the scripture saith, whosoever believeth on him shall not be ashamed." They shall not be disappointed.

The Gospel has the power to save every human being without distinction. The qualification is not race, nationality, intellect, or education, but belief. The Gospel of Jesus Christ is what a person must place their faith in. To believe is to receive Jesus Christ as presented in the Gospel.

Believers must always remember that the purpose of the Gospel of Jesus Christ is salvation, the eternal salvation of men and women.

Football fans who love the Dallas Cowboys or the Washington Redskins will talk about them. In some cases, they will argue with others about the status of their favorite team. If you love Jesus so much, you should tell somebody about him?

Jesus commanded us in Matthew 28:19, "To go into all the world." The world wants to hear "good news." And our message of the gospel is *good news*. It says, "God so loved the world;" that's good news. The good news says, "Jesus Christ died for our sins on the cross." It says, "Jesus Christ was buried and rose again on the third day. It says, "For as many as received him to them gave he power to become the sons of God.

The only message that we really have today is that Jesus saves; that is the good news. Your friends and family members need to hear from you that Jesus saves!

Disciples Are "Born Again"

On the evening after his resurrection, Jesus appeared to his disciples and gave them his Great Commission in two parts: (1) their new birth by the Spirit, and (2) he sent of them into the world to share his Gospel.

Jesus himself was conceived by the Holy Spirit (Matthew 1:18, 20). He told his disciples that they, too, would have an experience of being indwelt by the Holy Spirit. In John 14:17, he said to them, "The Spirit...dwells *with* you and *will be in* you." Before Jesus's death and resurrection, the Holy Spirit was *with* his disciples. But immediately after his resurrection from the dead, Jesus imparted the Spirit literally *into* his faithful disciples ("He shall be *in* you"). This was the moment when those disciples were "born again" by the Holy Spirit; they received the experience that Jesus had spoken of in John 3:3, 6–7: "You must be born again."

The second thing was, along with the new birth, Jesus "sent" them to do his work. Some Christians have the wrong outlook of being born again. They are hoping for an immediate "rapture" out of the world. But Jesus said quite the opposite: "My prayer is not that you take them out of the world... As you sent me into the world, I have sent them into the world" (John 17:15, 18). We have kingdom work to do! There is a world that needs the message of Jesus Christ, and he is sending us into that world with the message of his grace and salvation from our sins.

The Holy Spirit miraculously washes and changes us by giving new life, new understanding, new desires, and new power. Titus 3:5

says, "He saved us not because of righteous things we had done, but because of his mercy. He saved us through the washing of rebirth and renewal by the Holy Spirit." Born again means we're born into a new life with Christ.

Born again can be translated "born anew" or "born from above." It is like a new creation of the Spirit" which means that a person must be born again by the Holy Spirit using the Word of God. Jesus was speaking about a spiritual birth, but Nicodemus was thinking only of a physical birth. "Therefore, if any man be in Christ, he is a new creation; old things are passed away, behold, all things are become new" (2 Corinthians 5:17). When a person becomes born again, they receive the character of God. Christians are not just good moral people, but we are new creatures.

Jesus Christ meant born from above by the use of water, which is the Word of God, and the Holy Spirit making it real—confirming in the heart of the sinner this saving grace. Throughout the Bible, water is used to symbolize the Word of God. Therefore, I believe that "born of water and of the Spirit" means that a person must be born again by the Holy Spirit using the Word of God.

Just as there are two parents for physical birth, so there are two "parents" for spiritual birth: the Spirit of God (John 3:5) and the Word of God (James 1:18; 1 Peter 1:23–25).

Disciples Are Salt and Light

Jesus used salt as a symbol of discipleship. In Matthew 5:13, Jesus tells us, "Ye are the salt of the earth, but if the salt lost its savor, with what shall it be salted?" Salt was one of the most common substances in the ancient world. Roman soldiers were paid in salt and would revolt if they didn't get their full payment. Our English word "salary" comes from the Latin *salarium* which literally means "salt money." And our expression, "That man is not worth his salt," is a reminder of the high value that salt had in biblical times.

But what did Jesus mean by this statement, "You are the *salt* of the Earth?" It is the silent witness of the Christian believer. It is the influence the believer has over other people's lives to season and preserve for eternal life. Jesus Christ is saying, let your influence season people's life for the kingdom. Salt changes things! It only takes a little salt to flavor a whole community, a whole neighborhood, a whole workplace. The whole issue of salt is the seasoning, the influence. It is often said, "The salt is no good if it never leaves the salt shaker, and it becomes only a piece of decoration on the kitchen table."

We deny the salt function when we fail to mingle with people that are lost; we deny the function of the salt when we fail to be kind, merciful, to be a peacemaker. To deny the salt function is to deny the principles of the kingdom of God. We are not to draw away from society; we are not of the world, but we live in the world. And if we as *salt* don't rub against those who have no flavor, those who are perishing, who will?

The distinctive quality of salt is not its color because many things are white. It is not its texture because many things are granulated. The distinctive quality of salt is its taste, its saltiness. The distinctive quality of discipleship is its sacrifice. Discipleship without sacrifice is like salt without its flavor; it is useless and worthless.

Salt gives us strength. You can't live without sodium in your diet. Without it, your body quickly weakens. That's one reason the Romans gave their soldiers salt. They knew that putting salt on their vegetables would give them needed strength.

Salt creates a thirst. As salt, we have the opportunity to promote a thirst for Jesus Christ in the world. The only thing that will quench their spiritual thirst is the Living Water—Jesus Christ.

Jesus said, "You are the salt." He didn't say you might be the salt of the earth, or you ought to be the salt of the earth. No, you are the salt. We are called to be a people of influence—not to judge them, not to dominate people, not to ignore people—but to provide opportunity to serve them.

Salt works silently, but you see it operating. Things are delicious without ever seeing the salt. You don't have to preach a sermon to be salt, but your influence, your love, your peace, your meekness, your mercy will influence someone else's life.

You are the salt of the earth. If you are not functioning as God intends you to function, then you are worthless in bringing glory to his name or being a preserving influence in the world. He says in Matthew 5:13, "But if the salt has lost its savor, with what shall it be salted? It is *therefore good for nothing*, but to be cast out, and to be trodden under the foot of men."

Light has been a symbol of God's divine presence. Jesus said, "I am the light of the world. He who follows me shall not walk in darkness, but have the light of life" (John 8:12). "The Lord is my light and my salvation; whom shall I fear? The Lord is the strength of my life; of whom shall I be afraid?" (Psalm 27:1). To be the light of the world means illuminating the darkness so that others may see reality.

Functions of light:

- *Light exposes darkness.* Darkness is expelled as soon as it is hit by the light. People are not aware of the darkness they live in if they don't see the light. "The people who were sitting in darkness saw a great light" (Matthew 4:16). The question is, does my life help people see more clearly?
- *Light serves a guide.* Airport runways help planes see their runway by the lights. When we try to drive in the dark without light, it is dangerous. We are guides to people who are in darkness. Jesus is the true light, and we are reflectors of his light. John the Baptist said, "He was not that Light, but was sent to bear witness of that Light. That was the true Light, which gives light to every man coming into the world" (John 1:6–9). We are light, and our purpose is to make God known. If an unbeliever comes in contact with us, he or she ought to see in us the reflection of God's character. They ought to hear from our lips the truth of God and that which is good. We are to be proclaiming the truth of his salvation unto them.
- *Light is to be seen.* The light of every Christian must be visible. Jesus used the metaphor of a *lampstand* because he expects his followers to be seen by the world. They must give light so that men may glorify the Father in heaven. No one lights a light only to put it under a basket or earthen vessel; we are to let our light shine to the maximum. Every disciple must need to be a light at all times. Our light shines, not that people will be attracted to us, but to the *true light* who is Jesus Christ.

We are to dispel darkness. The whole issue with the light is to be a light in the darkness. Jesus said, "You are the light of the world." That means every Christian is a light to help others find salvation. But you don't have light of your own any more than the moon has light without the sun, or a light bulb has light without being connected to a power source. Jesus Christ is our power source, and when we are connected to him, we become light to the whole world.

True disciples cannot overlook the fact that we are light, and that we have a responsibility to walk as children of light (Ephesians 5:7–9). This means that goodness, righteousness, and truth ought to characterize the way we live our lives as believers.

Disciples Are Witnesses
of Jesus Christ

The dictionary defines the word "witness" as "one who has seen or heard something" and "one who furnishes evidence." A witness is someone who can say, "I know this is true." In a court of law, a witness swears on a Bible and promises to tell the truth, the whole truth, and nothing but the truth. Witnesses tell the truth, and if they are good witnesses, that is all they do.

When we received Jesus Christ as our Lord and Savior, our first reaction might have been to tell our best friend all about our salvation, that is, to witness to them of Christ. Witnessing for Christ is simply telling others what we have personally seen and experienced of the Lord Jesus. We are to witness for our Lord and Savior throughout our lives on this earth.

In Isaiah 48:10, God said, "You are my witnesses." God has no other plans for spreading the Gospel other than us—his people, his church. There is no plan B. There is no backup plan. There is no contingency plan. "You are my witnesses!" The church's mission is to get to know God and help other folks to find him too!

Jesus has commanded that his disciples be his witnesses. In Acts 1:8, he told the disciples, "But you will receive power when the Holy Spirit comes on you; and you will be my witnesses in Jerusalem, and in all Judea and Samaria, and to the ends of the earth." This is a command. Jesus did not say you might be my witnesses. Jesus did not say be a witness if it is convenient. He said you *shall*, you *will be*, my witnesses. The word "you" in this verse is in the plural. It means all of us. Not just the pastor and ministers. He didn't just call you to be a preacher, but he also called you to be a witness. He didn't call you to be a gossiper/slanderer; he called you to be a witness. He didn't call you only to holiness, but he called you to be a witness. Jesus says to tell the people everywhere you go; tell them about me.

Two things really stand out in this verse: (1) The Holy Spirit empowers the disciples, and (2) Spirit-filled disciples witness about Jesus. We need the Holy Spirit's power and initiative in our evangelism. We shouldn't ever think of going out into the world without the Holy Spirit's power and guidance.

What did God leave you on earth to do? Did he leave us on earth to sing praises to him? We can do that in heaven. Did he leave us on earth to pray to him? We can pray in heaven. When you think about it, there is one main thing you can do on earth that you will never do in heaven: you can tell a lost sinner about Jesus Christ. There are no sinners in heaven, so if you're going to tell them the Good News, you've got to do it while you're here on earth.

Just before he returned to heaven, Jesus gave his followers the authority to share the Gospel through the Holy Spirit who makes us witnesses. What he said to them, he also says to us. He left us on the earth that we might be his witnesses. A witness is "one who has seen or heard something" and "one who can furnish evidence." A witness is someone who can say, "I know this is true." A disciple is a witness who tells on the basis of personal experience what he or she knows to be the truth about Jesus Christ.

Jesus does not send angels to proclaim his name, and he does not flash the gospel in lightning across the skies. He uses people like us to convince other people like us to believe in him. We are Jesus' witnesses; we are his evidence to convince an unbelieving world. God has no other plan.

The English word for witness is the word "martyr" which comes from the Greek word *martures*. This means being loyal to the end if you are going to witness for Jesus Christ. It will make you unpopular in the world. You might be passed over for a promotion on your job, or you may lose friend. Many believers in the early church chose death rather than deny the name of our Lord Jesus Christ. Are you willing to die for Christ? Are you willing to live for him?

As believers, we are called to testify for Jesus—his life, death, resurrection, and his teachings. We are called to testify to the Word of God and to the testimony of Jesus Christ, and to all the things that we have seen in Jesus. We are to bear witness to him!

They know who Jesus is. The witnesses of Jesus know who Jesus is. We must know his deity, that Jesus is divine. In 1 Timothy 3:16, it says, "God was manifest in the flesh." This clearly declares that Jesus is God in the flesh, that with his humanity is also his divinity. He alone has this dual personality or nature. He is both, as the Bible speaks of him, as the "the Son of Man" and "the Son of God."

We know that Jesus is the Son of God—his divine nature, the second person of the Godhead. We know him as the Son of Man—his racial name, which depicts his nature as a human being. We also know him as the Son of David—his Jewish name, which depicts his nature as the promised Messiah, the Christ. Because of this unique nature, Jesus alone qualifies to become the *mediator* between God and man. He's the only bridge that can bring reconciliation between a sinner and a Holy God.

We not only know about him, but we know him personally; we have experienced him (1 John 1:2, 4:14). We have walked with him. We have seen and heard him. We have the testimony in our hearts (1 John 5:10).

You can know a lot about someone without knowing the person himself. But you need to know Christ personally. You need to know who he claimed to be—eternal God in human flesh. You must know some of the things he did and taught. You need to understand that he died on the cross for your sins, and that he was raised bodily from the dead.

They know who they are. We not only know who Jesus is, but we also know who we are and what we are called to do. Disciples are Christ's followers—people who are fully committed to obeying Jesus Christ in every part of their lives. Jesus Christ is not just a part of their lives, but Jesus Christ is their life. The Apostle Paul said to the church at Philippi, "For me to live is Christ And to die is gain"

(Philippians 1:21). By this, Paul meant that his life was wrapped up in Jesus Christ, in following Christ, and in fellowship with Christ. It means growing to love Christ with all of my heart, soul, mind, and strength. It means submitting all of my thoughts, emotions, words, and deeds to the lordship of Christ, to please him in all respects.

We understand we are his witnesses. In Acts 1:8, Jesus says to his disciples, "You shall be *my* witnesses." As a witness for Christ, the disciple's life is a key part of his or her witness. As a new creation, the way your new faith shows itself in your conduct is the greatest testimony you have. This means your habits and lifestyle should reflect a life given over to Jesus Christ.

It is exciting to witness and share your faith in Jesus Christ with others—to tell how Jesus Christ changed your own life. There is power in a simple and honest personal testimony.

Jesus charges us as his witnesses: *you, as my witness, shall bear witness to me and tell the truth and nothing but the truth about me to all the world.* That is our call. That is our charge. We know who we are.

They know what to tell. We also know what to tell—tell the truth. To testify to the truth is the bottom line for any witness. Truth determines the validity of the testimony. There's always a danger of perjury. But a true witness must tell the truth.

In 1 John 5:11–12, it sums up the truth about Jesus this way: "God gave us eternal life, and this life is in His Son. Whoever has the Son has life; whoever does not have the Son of God does not have life."

That's the testimony. That's our story to tell to the world. Christ's witnesses know who Jesus is, they know who they are, and they know what to tell. If you know Jesus, you can tell about what he has done for you. You can share how he's changed your life. You can tell how he guides you, day by day, how he gives you strength to face your trials and courage to conquer your fears. You can tell how he found you in your sin and gave you a brand-new life.

The Mandate to Make Disciples

The word "mandate" means a command from a higher authority. The *basis* of our mandate is found in Matthew 28:18, "Jesus said, all authority in heaven and on earth has been given to me. Therefore go." This indicates that evangelism is not "A Great Suggestion," but it is the "The Great Commission." There is no higher mandate, no greater authority in heaven or earth than the authority of Jesus Christ. He is the ultimate authority; no one has the authority to change, alter, or delete his commands. He is Lord; we do what he says. He determines the destiny of every single person in the world and has commanded us to go and speak and act in his name. What a high honor it is to be called his disciples.

Christ has all authority so that we might go to all the nations and teach all things, which Jesus commanded for all of our days.

Jesus Christ gave his church a mandate, a command to move out of the comfortable pews and go and do the work of missions. He said, "Therefore, go." Or to translate it from the Greek, it says, therefore, "as you are going" or "since you are going." Making disciples involves going. Therefore, *going* represents something disciples do continually. We must go to these unreached people and share the life-giving Gospel of Jesus Christ.

Christ told them to "go," which is an outcome of his authority and of his statement that he will be with them always. Because of his continuous presence, it could translate as "go with me."

We cannot "go" if we are sitting still. We cannot "go" if we stay where we are. We cannot "go" if we do not make a move. As you are passing through this world, you should be carrying the Gospel with you. You should be sharing it with everyone that you meet. We are not to wait for the world to come to our door, but we are to go to the world.

The famous boxer, Muhammad Ali, made a statement after he won the world heavyweight championship his first time. He said, "I shook up the world, I shook up the world." That was the command of Jesus to his disciples more than 2000 years ago—for us to go and shake up the world. The first disciples were accused of doing just that in Acts 17:6. It says, "These that have turned the world upside down."

Many churches today have what is called the "Martha Mentality" found in Luke 10:38–42. Martha was so worried about her housework that she didn't recognize that Jesus was there in the house. She was more concerned about the lamb roasting in the oven than she was about The Lamb of God sitting in her living room. We are so worried about getting church work done that we are missing out on getting *kingdom* work done.

Churches and their leaders must recognize that reaching the lost is *kingdom* work, not just church work.

Evangelism is taking the church to the people; it is not bringing people to the church. Evangelism involves going—"Go ye therefore." And as you are going, present the Gospel and bring the unbeliever to Christ.

"Elvis has left the building!" was a phrase used after Elvis Presley finished his concerts. It was used to disperse the crowd that lingered around hoping for an Elvis encore.

That should be the announcement at the end of every worship service and of every fellowship or Bible study; of every prayer meeting and every church business meeting: "The church has left the building."

Jesus was placing the emphasis on his strategy to "make disciples." Notice that he did not say, go and build church buildings or worship centers. He did not say go appoint bishops. He did not say, go and establish theological colleges, missionary societies, or charitable institutions. These things are useful, but they are not the priority. The mandate is "making disciples" who will reproduce themselves.

The mandate of The Great Commission is to "Go," and this is a word of action! There are two ways we can do this:

- It involves *our lifestyle*. Read Matthew 5:13–16. Like salt, our life should create a thirst in people for the Lord. Our joy, our peace, our differences from the world should cause them to want to know why we are like we are. Our lives should be like a great spotlight which directs its beam toward Jesus. If he is the focus of our lives, men will see him lived out through our lives day by day!

- It involves *our lips*. We are told to "teach." That word has the idea of "making disciples or to instruct." Making disciples means instructing new believers on how to follow Jesus Christ, how to submit to Jesus as Lord, and how to carry out his mission of reaching the lost.

We are to live the right kind of life, but we are also told to share our faith. We are to tell a lost world what Jesus did for us when he saved us and what he can do for them, if they will trust him as we did. It's not enough to just show it; we must also say it! Mark 16:15 instructs us to "Go ye into all the world, and preach the gospel to every creature." The word "preach" is a present voice tense, active voice tense, imperative voice tense. The imperative voice means it is a command. The active voice tense means to be involved in carrying out the command. The present voice tense means that it is something we should be doing all the time. The word "preach" comes from a word that means "to herald." Like a king's herald, we are to pass through the highways and byways of life, lifting our voices to declare the Gospel of grace all the time!

The Message to Make Disciples

The gospel message is more than just an announcement or a basic truth to be impressed upon unbelievers. Jesus tells his followers to share a specific message: "to observe all things whosoever I have commanded you." As you go and as we tell the world about Jesus, the message we are to share is very clear. We are to share the Gospel.

We are living in a day when the message of the church is changing. Many churches and denominations are moving away from the message of salvation through the blood of Jesus. Today, they are preaching the message of prosperity, telling people how God will bless them if they just ask in Jesus's name. It's the name-it-and-claim-it generation—people claiming blessings in Jesus's name, and they are not saved.

The Gospel's message that the church need to preach is the one that will bring people to salvation by telling them who Jesus is and what Jesus has done. Therefore, the Gospel message is more than just an announcement, more than a basic truth to be impressed upon sinners. This message is also applicable to the believing church member.

Our message is not a message about our church or our denomination. It is not about the preacher, our standards of dress or music, nor our style of worship. All of those are important, but none of them can save a lost, hell-bound soul. Our message is a simple message. Our message is telling people the good news about Jesus Christ and the free gift of salvation that he alone offers. It is a message of hope to the hurting, of life to the dead, and of peace to the tormented. Our message points a lost world to Jesus Christ and to him alone. It does not preach salvation through religion or ritual, "For by grace are ye saved through faith" (Ephesians 2:8–9). It holds Jesus up as the final and only solution to the problem of sin. It preaches a transcendent message that speaks to all social classes, all races, and all sinners. It is a message that calls everyone to repent and believe the Gospel.

As a body of believers called the church, the message is not about us. It is not about the singing or the preaching; nor is it about our gift, our title, or our position. It is all about Jesus Christ.

The message is called the Gospel, and "it is the power of God unto salvation, to the Jew first and also to the Greek" (Romans 1:16). This is the central message of the people of God. It is a message that every person in the world needs to hear. It is a message that is universal in its application—a message that has the potential to change every life and every eternity that falls under its power (John 1:11–12).

In his letter to the church in Romans, Paul commended the congregation in Rome because their "faith" is spoken of throughout the whole world (Romans 1:8). The congregation was already established and apparently thriving. Yet Paul says, "So, as much as is in me, I am ready to preach the gospel to you who are in Rome also" (Romans 1:15).

Jesus did not say: "Teach them all the things I have commanded you." But he said: "Teach them to *observe* all the things I have commanded you." To observe a command means to "conform one's action" to that command, to obey it, or keep it.

God's message is called "The Gospel of the Kingdom of God" because this is the goal. He wants us always to focus on. In the message, he wants it to come immediately to mind that we are headed toward his Kingdom. We not only have to know that the kingdom is coming, but we must prepare ourselves for it.

The Gospel message that we proclaim is the "power of God unto salvation" (Romans 1:15). Jesus Christ has given us a message that will break down the walls of sin in the lives of people and reconcile them to God. This message includes everything that is necessary to call, teach, correct, and motivate a person to receive salvation and inherit the kingdom. The true gospel is the complete revelation of God to man. It includes everything contained in the Bible.

The Mission to Make Disciples

In what is known as the Great Commission, Jesus tells us that we are to "Go…and teach all nations." In Mark 16:15, Jesus says, "Go ye into all the world, and preach the gospel to every creature." In Acts 1:8, Jesus says, "But ye shall receive power, after that the Holy Ghost is come upon you: and ye shall be witnesses unto me both in Jerusalem, and in all Judaea, and in Samaria, and unto the uttermost part of the earth."

The church is a community with a mission. The church's mission is to glorify God by proclaiming the Gospel to the lost and making Christlike disciples who make Christlike disciples. The entire church is given the responsibility to carry out this mission. The mission is not simply for specialty groups or experts. Neither is missions simply an overseas trip.

Missions mean sending. A missionary is one sent with the message to preach the good news to the lost. Jesus said to his disciples to go into the world. To do missions, we must endeavor to get out of our comfort zones in order to win others for the Lord. It must be noted that every mission-minded church must be a sending and a going church. This is not a divine suggestion that Jesus gives to his church, but it is a command.

The command to make disciples is to every believer; you are the messengers! He did not tell us to put up a sign, and they will come. He did not say send out letters and e-mails, and they will come. He did not tell us to put it in the newspapers, and they will come. No, this is one on one; it is up close and personal. You are the messenger!

The church is on its mission to introduce people in every place to Jesus Christ. As the church makes disciples, people can worship, trust, follow, and obey Jesus as their Savior and Lord. Our mission is to put him on display to every nation.

We are told to "teach." The word teach carries the idea of "making disciples or to instruct." The command to teach is not just telling them what Jesus has commanded, but teaching them obedience to what Jesus has commanded. The truths of the Bible are to be obeyed. Those who obey his teaching demonstrate a saving knowledge of Jesus Christ. If Jesus is your Savior, then he is your Lord. If he is not your Lord, he is not your Savior. Making disciples means instructing new believers on how to follow Jesus Christ, how to submit to Jesus as Lord, and how to carry out his mission of reaching the lost.

During my final year of high school, I chose to enroll in the agriculture class. Each student in the class had to choose a project to help determine their complete grade. I chose to raise chickens.

I purchased a chicken coop and twelve baby chickens and, for three months, watched them grow. At the end of three months, I noticed the chickens began to fight one another, pecking constantly at each other. One day, I looked into the coop, and one chick was dead.

I talked to the agriculture teacher, and he informed me that I needed to release the chickens into the yard to allow them space to grow and develop.

After doing this, I noticed the chickens were no longer fighting with one another and were even healthier.

I believe this also applies to many of our local churches. Many church members are fighting and fussing inside the church because they have a need to be released. The inward focus has not allowed them to be free to grow and to use their gifts.

The work of evangelism will give them the outward focus they need to keep from pecking one another like chickens.

Those who are followers of Jesus Christ are a sent people. Jesus explained this sending in John 20:21 when he said, "As the Father has sent me, so I send you."

When Jesus spoke these words to his disciples, he was also speaking to us today. He was telling exactly what he expected his church to do in his physical absence.

Jesus meant that his disciples should replicate themselves. Matthew's Gospel teaches that Jesus had put years into developing his successors, and Jesus wanted his disciples to do in others what he had done in them.

This is our mission—to "make disciples" as we are going about our daily lives. Our mission is wherever we find ourselves at the moment—whether it be at work, on vacation, in a restaurant, or in the family. Christian parents are to make disciples of their children. Christian employers are to make disciples of their employees. Employees are to make disciples of their fellow employees.

Jesus is telling us very clearly that our mission is to every person in the world. That our mission field is the entire world. Jesus may call us from among them to leave the country and reach a certain people, or he may ask us to financially support those whom he has called to reach those in other parts of the world. However, he may never call us to go to a foreign land to tell the story of salvation, but he does expect us to tell it where we live. He expects us to reach out to all people without regard to their ethnic heritage, race, past, lifestyle, economic standing, etc. If they are sinners, they are candidates to hear the message of the cross. If they are lost, they need a Savior. If they do not know him, they need to, and we have been authorized and commanded to reach them!

The Method to Make Disciples

Baptism is the way the new disciple is identified as being a follower of Christ. No, baptism didn't make the person a Christian; it just showed they are a Christian. Baptism is a symbol of the believer following after Jesus Christ. It is through baptism one could be assured that a disciple was made. It is their initiation into the kingdom of God. Jesus told them to baptize the believers. After they have won folk to Jesus, then they must baptize them. Those which were being discipled were fully identifying with and falling under the lordship of Jesus. If we fail to baptize, then we disobey the command of the Lord.

This word, baptize, is the Greek word *baptizo* which means to immerse, to plunge, to submerge, or to dip into something. The descriptions of baptism in the New Testament indicates that people went down into the water to be immersed and not that water was brought to them to be poured or sprinkled on them. When Jesus was baptized, he came up out of the water. When the Ethiopian eunuch was ready to be baptized, they went down into the water and came up out of the water.

Baptism is a step of publicly announcing the decision to be emptied of self for Christ, a sacrificial devotion to Christ that flows from a heart of love for him.

Water baptism is like a funeral. It is an act of faith in which we testify, both to God and to the world, that the person we were before is dead and buried, and we are raised as a new creation in Christ. When I got baptized, it gave other folk a picture of me dying to my old life. The old Joe was dead. So what do you do with a dead man? My baptism indicated I was dead and was buried in Christ. Romans 6:11 says, "Likewise, reckon ye also yourselves to be dead indeed unto sin, but alive unto God through Jesus Christ our Lord." The devil was the only one moaning at my baptismal burial. The devil was crying at my baptism because he hated to see my old life die. He knew that I had served him well. I thought I saw tears in his eyes when the people started singing, "Take me to the waters to be baptized."

Baptism is not a saving grace but a sanctifying grace. It's a prescribed step of obedience for those who are in Christ. Baptism is also a picture of the believer's present life. It pictures death to our old life and being raised up to walk in newness of life. It shows his or her belief in the resurrection of Jesus Christ. Jesus Christ did not stay in the grave. He died, and he was buried, but on Sunday morning, he rose from the grave. When a believer goes down into the water, the minister puts that person under the water but then raises them back up out of the water. This shows that their old life was buried but was raised to a new life in Jesus Christ.

We practice baptism to follow the example of Christ. When Jesus began his earthly ministry, he asked John the Baptist to baptize him (Matthew 3:13). Jesus, in his baptism, was publicly declaring that he was conforming to the will of God, to be the suffering servant in Isaiah 53:3–9.

The baptism of Jesus Christ was the inauguration of his ministry. As followers of Christ, we inaugurate our journey of faith by walking in obedience to Christ's example in baptism. We get baptized to follow the example of Christ.

We practice baptism to obey the command of Christ (Matthew 28:19). Baptism is a command from Jesus, not an option. Baptize them into the household of faith and teach them to obey all that Jesus Christ has commanded. It is an act that God requires of every believer. In fact, Jesus said in Mark 16:16, "He that believeth and is baptized shall be saved." To say it like that, Jesus saw baptism as being something very important.

When we follow the command of Christ and the example of Christ and step into the water in obedience in baptism, we are physically declaring and demonstrating the Gospel of Jesus Christ.

You never read of an unbaptized Christian in the Bible. In fact, baptism would immediately follow a person's salvation. They didn't see it as something to be delayed or put off.

Notice in Matthew 28:19, Jesus said, "Baptizing them in the name of the Father, and of the Son, and of the Holy Ghost." All three persons of the Godhead were present when Jesus was baptized by John the Baptist. When we get baptized, it is to remind us that all three are there with us in our baptism. It reminds us that God the Father shall supply all our needs according to his riches in glory by Christ Jesus. In the name of the Son reminds us that Jesus Christ, the Son, is our Savior. "For as many as received him to them gave he power to become the sons of God, even to them that believed on his name." In the name of the Holy Spirit reminds us that the Spirit is our Comforter. That he is living in every believer. So when life confronts us with troubles and sorrows and sickness and pain, or when Satan attacks us without warning, we can say, "Greater is he that is in me than he that is in the world."

Water baptism versus baptism in the Spirit

Bible scholar, J.C. Ryle, wrote: "When you get baptized in the Holy Spirit, you get cleansed by God, and he will come into our hearts. It is a baptism, not of the body, but of the heart. It is good to be baptized into the visible Church; but it is far better to be baptized by the Spirit into that Church which is made up of true believers."

Baptism in the Holy Spirit can be defined as at the moment of salvation; the Holy Spirit places a believer into permanent union with Jesus Christ and with other believers into the body of Christ. The baptism of the Spirit is given to all believers alike, because all believers are baptized by the Holy Spirit, and all believers have been baptized into Christ (1 Corinthians 12:13). Baptism in the Holy Spirit means we are risen with Jesus Christ to the newness of life (Romans 6:4), and that we should exercise our spiritual gifts to keep the body of Christ functioning properly as stated in 1 Corinthians 12:13.

Baptism in the Holy Spirit does two things. First, it identifies us spiritually with the death and resurrection of Christ, uniting us with him. Second, baptism in the Holy Spirit joins us to the body of Christ and identifies us and unites us with other believers.

When you get baptized in water, it is a symbol that you are being purified by God, but when you get baptized by the Holy Spirit, God brings you into his kingdom.

Water baptism does not make you a believer, but it shows that you are already one! Water baptism does not "save" you; only your faith in Christ does that.

The Mentor to Make Disciples

Jesus chose twelve men to become his disciples. He was their mentor, and he prepared them to carry on his ministry after he had ascended back to the Father in Heaven.

Today, Jesus is still our mentor. He doesn't send us into this lost world without any resources. He doesn't expect us to accomplish this Great Commission in our own power. In fact, these verses give us the greatest resources we have as witnesses of the Gospel.

We have the *promise of his presence*: "Lo, I am with you always." The purpose of Jesus's constant presence is so that we will have all that we need to fulfill Jesus's Great Commission: to see the glory of God among the nations. When you are sharing the Gospel with a friend, a family member, or even a total stranger, the Lord himself is right there with you. He will help you, enable you, embolden you, and use you if you will obey him and share the Gospel with others. You will never share the Gospel alone if you are a child of God!

Jesus is present with all believers by the Holy Spirit who lives within us. Therefore, he will help the believer to say what needs to be said when the witnessing opportunity presents itself. He said in Matthew 10:19–20, "But when they deliver you up, take no thought how or what ye shall speak: for it shall be given you in that same hour what ye shall speak. For it is not ye that speak, but the Spirit of your Father which speaketh in you." This is clear that he is talking about being arrested for the faith. When that occurs, he will give the words to speak. The same principle applies to our witness. When we witness, we are on trial for our faith. He will give us the words we need when the time comes.

We have the *promise of his power* : "All power in Heaven and earth is given unto me." He also says, "But ye shall receive power, after that the Holy Ghost is come upon you: and ye shall be witnesses unto me" (Acts 1:8). When we are faithful to share his Gospel message, we can be confident God will use his message for his glory. He will take our words, and he will attach his power to them. The Spirit of God will take our efforts, and he will use the words that we share to convict the hearts of the lost.

Evangelism as a Lifestyle

Lifestyle evangelism combines proclaiming Jesus (Romans 1:16) with living a life that shows others the difference Jesus makes. Lifestyle evangelism calls Christians to live an attractive, winsome, holy life that captures the attention of family, friends, neighbors, and coworkers to earn a chance to share the gospel. Lifestyle evangelism is all about relationships. People do not trust those who have flawed characters. Good character will open up doors for lasting relationships with those around you.

In every area of a disciple's life, he or she should look for opportunities to share the gospel and do it! This implies that our lives should be lived in such a way that others are curious about our faith, and that we need to be able and be willing to share our faith with others. Disciples should make evangelism a way of life. The call to make disciples is given to every Christian, not just to pastors or church leaders. Every believer is challenged, not only to be a disciple of Jesus Christ, but also to make disciples.

The life that we live on a day-to-day basis should reflect our personal relationship with Christ. The manner in which we carry ourselves should *influence* those around us to "want what we have." We make disciples when we invite people to walk with us as we follow Jesus, grow in faith, and strive to be faithful servants. Disciples are life-long learners. We make disciples when we invite people to join with us in learning more about God, our world, ourselves, and the teachings of Jesus.

There are many people who are critical of lifestyle evangelism today, saying lifestyle evangelism falls short or allows Christians to avoid sharing the gospel verbally. But true lifestyle evangelism requires telling the Good News in the context of personal relationship. Other strategies, such as tracts and media, are more direct but less personal.

The Scriptures describes evangelism in the life of believers to be "natural and normal." Not just a program that we conform to. When evangelism is just a program that we adhere to, then it can separate us from discipleship in our daily lives.

The goal for every disciple in lifestyle evangelism is to share the Gospel through both actions and words. If all you are being is a good example to your neighbors, coworkers, and friends, you are not doing any evangelism. We witness with both our life and with our lips. Open up your mouth and proclaim the name of Christ.

Disciples in the early church talked about their faith; it was part of their daily life. You might say that faith in Christ overflows into their conversation. I believe that they spoke of the change that Jesus Christ made in their life and use that in helping people follow Jesus.

Don Whitney made the following statement in his book on evangelism as a discipline: "Evangelism is a natural overflow of the Christian life. We should all be able to talk about what the Lord has done for us and what he means to us. But evangelism is also a discipline in that we must discipline ourselves to get into the context of evangelism, that is, we must not just wait for witnessing opportunities to happen."

Jesus said in Matthew 5:16, "Let your light shine before men, that they may see your good deeds and praise your Father in heaven." To "let" your light shine before others means more than simply "Don't do anything to keep your light from shining." Think of his exhortation as "Let there be the light of good works shining in your life; let there be the evidence of God-honoring change radiating from you. Let it begin! Make room for it."

We are saved for good works. According to Ephesians 2:10, we are God's workmanship. The Greek word for "workmanship" is *poiema*, from which we get our word "poem." It means "a work of

153

art, a masterpiece." In Christ, we receive God's grace through our faith and become his work of art. We are God's workmanship to do his good works. God has saved us to serve. People should be able to see our good works and glorify our Heavenly Father (Matthew 5:16).

They should see that we are: adorning or decorating ourselves; to make ourselves more pleasing to God (1 Timothy 2:9–10).

Evangelizing Others According to Romans 10:9–10

Making disciples means instructing new believers on how to follow Jesus Christ, how to submit to Jesus as Lord, and how to carry out his mission of reaching the lost. The church should teach every believer how to present God's plan of salvation

Romans 10:9–10 says, "That if thou shalt confess with thy mouth the Lord Jesus, and shalt believe in thine heart that God hath raised him from the dead, thou shalt be saved. For with the heart man believeth unto righteousness; and with the mouth confession is made unto salvation."

One of the greatest danger for the church today is assuming the salvation of people who simply claim the label "Christian" or those who are involved in church activities. Not being careful about who we consider to be "born again." According to Romans 10:9–10, there can be no "secret" Christians. The very act of becoming a Christian requires us to confess publicly that we have accepted Jesus Christ as our Savior and have placed our faith in his shed blood to atone for our sins.

Jesus is Lord

The word Lord is the most common title for Jesus in the New Testament. God authenticated Jesus as both Lord and Christ. He announced his birth supernaturally with angels who told shepherds:

155

a Savior has been born to you. He is Christ the Lord (Luke 2:11). In Philippians 2:11, God declared Jesus to be "Lord." He is Lord of all creation. He is Lord of his church. He is Lord of the life of the individual Christian. If he is Lord, then he is worthy to be worshiped, loved, served, and obeyed. If He is Lord, then he is worthy of all our time, our talents, and our treasure. If He is Lord, then he deserves first place in our hearts and in our lives. If he is Lord, then he should be exalted, praised, and loved. If He is Lord, then let him be Lord of all. Many people are claiming Jesus is Lord, but they are not changing their lives to reflect that truth. Acts 10:36 tells us that if he is not Lord of all, then he is not Lord at all!

The Greek word for "Lord" is *kurios*. The word "Lord" have meanings. It means the one to whom a person or thing has supremacy or belongs. It is the one who has the power of deciding what to do with such a thing. It is the one who has control of such a thing. It was a title of reverence given to superiors. It was a title that slaves used for their masters.

In Philippians 2:10, the bowing of the knee is a picture of a slave showing submission to his master. Therefore, this verse teaches that the bowing of the knee is a physical posture that is deserved and demanded in response to the exaltation of Christ. Whenever a dignitary or celebrity enters a room, the people will stand, applaud, and even cheer. But if Jesus Christ were to walk into that same room, no one would stand. No one would be able to stand. Every knee would bow down before him. Notice the verse says, "every knee should bow" and points the three places where the knee must bow before Christ: "in heaven and on earth and under the earth."

In Hebrews 1:3, it says, "When he by himself purged our sins, sat down on the right hand of the Majesty on high." Just what does it mean when the Bible says that Christ is seated at the right hand of the Father? It means that he has been given the place of honor in heaven. But it also means something else. The Old Testament priests didn't sit down while on duty in the temple because their work was never finished. They repeatedly made sacrifices which were necessary because of the priest's own sins and the sins of the people. But Jesus

Christ made one sacrifice that was all-sufficient then sat down. His atoning work was complete.

The word *kurios* is the Greek translation of the Hebrew name for God, Jehovah. When we confess Jesus Christ as Lord, we are saying that he is the God we worship, the King we obey, the Master we serve. If Jesus is our Lord, what are we in terms of our relationship to him? We are bond servants! A bond servant is a voluntary slave for life, and out of love for his master, one who gives up everything.

Romans 10:9–10 says, "That if thou shalt confess with thy mouth the Lord Jesus, and shalt believe in thine heart that God hath raised him from the dead, thou shalt be saved. For with the heart man believeth unto righteousness; and with the mouth confession is made unto salvation."

This is the fact of confessing Jesus being Lord, but when the saved person confesses that Jesus is Lord, it is not simply confessing this truth, but it is also acknowledging Jesus Christ is God. Thomas saw Jesus for himself. He was able to take in all that Christ risen from the dead meant, and this produced this confession with his mouth— my Lord and my God. It was faith and utter surrender to his Savior and God.

Jesus is Lord is the true essence of Christianity. Jesus is not just a part of God; He is not just a man sent from God; He is God. Jesus is God. He reveals God to us in human form, but that does not diminish his deity in any way. Jesus is revealed as the Creator and the Head of the Church, as the Savior of the world; all of those are expressions of the fact that he is God. The Lordship of Jesus Christ is built on this foundational truth: Jesus is God. Jesus didn't leave any doubt when he boldly proclaimed in John 10:30, "I and my Father are one."

Paul's letter was originally written to the Romans. So we must understand that according to Roman law, only Caesar could be called "Lord." In Latin, Roman believers would declare: "*Dominium Iesum*" (Jesus is Lord!). For a Roman citizen to publicly declare "Jesus is Lord" was a felony and that person prosecuted by death. They were beheaded or crucified and ripped apart by animals in the Roman arena. For believers living in Rome to say "Jesus is Lord," it was saying: "I am ready to be persecuted, tortured, and to die for the name of Jesus."

The Jews saw the word Lord as referring only to God. If a Jew believed in Jesus and claimed him as Lord, they were saying that Jesus was God (John 20:28). He is received as Lord before he becomes your Savior.

Our Lord is personal. His church doesn't worship an unknown God. We worship a Lord who personally redeemed us from our sins. We are in a powerful saving relationship with him. We know Jesus Christ, and we are consumed with love for him, and that love permeated all we do.

Jesus is Savior

The word Savior in the Greek word (*sōtēr*) means "one who makes safe, delivers, or preserves from harm." That's what Jesus came to this earth to do—to make us safe, to deliver us, and to preserve us from sin and hell and a life of sin and sorrow. "Savior" implies a need for help.

Help is not needed, that is, if we don't think we need a savior, if there are no threatening circumstances. But what threatens us spiritually, revealing our need for a Savior, are sin, Satan, judgment, and hell. We need to be saved from these things, to be delivered and preserved from them. To be saved, you must simply call upon the Lord in repentance and in faith (Romans 10:13). Calling upon the name of Jesus is the testimony of true faith in God.

Salvation is found in simply surrendering. Romans 10:9–10 tells us the entrance into salvation is as close to us as our own hearts and our own mouths. In these verses, Paul tells us that the heart and the mouth are involved in this matter of our salvation.

In these verses, Paul was speaking about the word of salvation being near to us, and we do not have to do some great thing to gain salvation. It is near us; it is in our mouth and in our heart by the word of faith being proclaimed to us. Those who hear this word and respond to it and understand it and receive it and, in faith, rest their souls upon it, find it in their hearts and minds in a very real way. Paul is not seeking to explain the ABC of the Gospel; nor is he teaching the truth as he has been doing in all the previous chapters. But Paul is describing the genuine experience of salvation in the believer.

According to Romans 10: 6–7, it isn't found in great signs; in these verses, Paul is quoting from Deuteronomy. He is saying that no one needs to look to Heaven or the earth for signs. Jesus has already come down from Heaven. An unsaved person is not required to search for Jesus in some scavenger hunt to find him. He has already come and made the way clear. Jesus had already taken care of everything for us!

Contrary to what our culture and other religions tell us, there are not multiple paths to God. There is only one way—Jesus Christ (John 14:6). He is an exclusive Savior. Acts 4:12 tells us, "Neither is there salvation in any other, for there is no other name under heaven given among men, whereby we must be saved."

Here are several things we need to consider about Jesus as our Savior:

- *Jesus Christ is a personal Savior.* A "personal relationship" can be defined as an experiential relationship between two persons that involves interaction and communication.

  The Christian faith has nothing to do with religion. It's all about relationship. It's all about the difference between knowing about God and knowing God. Knowing God is faith, and faith is a personal relationship with Jesus. A person must be "in Christ" to have a *personal relationship* with Christ. When you are baptized into Christ (Romans 6:3), then your relationship with Jesus Christ begins. Every spiritual blessing is "in Christ" (Ephesians 1:3). It is called "personal" because God knows and deals with each of us on a personal basis. Jesus said in John 10:27–28, "My sheep hear my voice, and I know them, and they follow me: And I give unto them eternal life; and they shall never perish, neither shall any man pluck them out of my hand."

  A personal relationship with Jesus Christ gives us the assurance of our salvation. Our salvation is made available to us by God's grace which we receive through our faith in the Lord Jesus Christ. The reason faith in Jesus Christ will save us is because the Word of God tells us that "Christ died for our sins" (1 Corinthians 15:3). The means of receiving God's forgiveness is our faith or trust in his Son, Jesus Christ.

A personal relationship with Jesus Christ gives us confidence for living. God wants us to have confidence as his children—not confidence in ourselves, but confidence in his Word and his will for our lives. Our confidence begins with the assurance of salvation. If we have received the Lord Jesus Christ as our personal Savior, the Word of God says in 1 John 3:1–3, "Now are we the sons and daughters of God." Once we have accepted Jesus Christ as our Savior, our relationship with God is restored. He begins a process of renewing our mind so that we may approve what is the good and acceptable and perfect will of God (Romans 12: 2).

- *Jesus Christ is a universal Savior.* John 3:16 tells us that "God so loved the world." God doesn't just love one set of people. He does not just love one particular nation or race. The scope of God's love covers the whole world—every nation, tribe, language, and people—all who come to him with repentant hearts, sorry for their sins, and believe that he is who he says he is, will receive his salvation.

  Jesus Christ lived and died because God loved you, and God loved your family, your friends, your neighbor, and even your enemy, and all the people you'll never have a chance to meet. God didn't ask the world whether or not it wanted to receive his love because we don't have a choice in the matter that God loves us—all of us—whether we like it or not, whether we want him to or not. He loves us unconditionally and loves us enough to sacrifice his son for us.

- *Jesus Christ is a comprehensive Savior.* Romans 8:29-30 makes it clear that our salvation, predestined from before the foundation of the world, includes not only justification and forgiveness of sins, but also God's commitment to transform us into the very image of his Son, and one day, when that process is complete, we will be glorified.

- *Jesus Christ is an all-powerful Savior.* Nothing can separate us from God's love. Jesus Christ's work on the cross sealed our salvation forever. As Romans 8:38–39 tells us, "For I am persuaded, that neither death, nor life, nor angels, nor principalities, nor powers, nor things present, nor things to come, nor height, nor depth, nor any other creature, shall be able to separate us from the love of God, which is in Christ Jesus our Lord."

The outward expression of salvation

The mouth. This is a confession with our mouth concerning Jesus. It is to confess Jesus is Lord.

Notice the phrase "with thy mouth." It is denoting a willingness to make a public declaration of your acceptance of these things and to be identified with Christ. Your confession with the mouth brings salvation (And with the mouth confession is made unto salvation). Confession is the outward sign of the inward grace of Christ working in your life. Literally, it is the admission that you need Christ. The confession with the mouth is a public acknowledgment elicited by an agreement with God in the inner being, the heart. What is acknowledged is not only that Jesus Christ is God, but you are proclaiming him your own personal Lord. We publicly confess with our mouth because we are willing to be made righteous, to become different, and to become just like Jesus.

The Word "confess" carries the idea of "saying the same thing about something." God wants the lost sinner to come to the place where that person can say the same thing about Jesus Christ that God the Father has already said about him. God wants us to come to the place where we are in agreement with everything the Bible says concerning the *person* and work of the Lord Jesus Christ. When a person confesses Jesus is Lord, it is not simply confessing this truth, but it is acknowledging Jesus as the one to whom he or she gives the total obedience and adoration of their whole being, with nothing held back. This confession is an expression of worship and adoration. It is an expression of surrender and bowing down in obedience. It is an expression of our realization of his glory and the wonder of his person and the feeling of his love shed abroad in our hearts.

All of these are essential to salvation! You cannot treat Jesus Christ like he is a buffet. You cannot select the part of him you like while rejecting the part of him you do not like. The mouth is required to confess the truth about *who* he is! So the first step is agreement with God about the *person* and work of the Lord Jesus Christ. Believing in your heart that a sin is wrong, or that Jesus is your Lord and Savior, is vitally important, but until you have confessed it with your mouth, your salvation is not complete. That act of confession is essential.

The confession with the mouth is a public acknowledgment of the agreement your soul has made with God. You not only acknowledge that Jesus Christ is God, but that you are personally accepting him as your Lord. The word Lord in the Greek language is the word *kurios*; it signifies someone who has power and authority over you. The Bible never separates the lordship of Christ from him as Savior.

The inward expression of salvation

The heart. This is the reality of our salvation. We believe in our hearts that God raised Jesus from the dead, and we lay hold by faith, in our deepest being, all that the resurrection implies. The faith in our hearts is that deep assurance in Jesus that he has saved us. Our inmost being, called the heart, is engaged with Jesus and filled with Jesus and what he is and what he has done. This is a deep engagement because of the realization of what this has achieved for us for all eternity, and the joy of what all that means.

In the days of the Old Testament, people saw the heart as the center of all thought—the deepest and most sacred part of man. It is the soul of a man, the inner man, this is where our thought and our will and our motives are generated. That's why Proverbs 4:23 says, "Watch over your heart with all diligence, for out of it flows the issues of life." It is with the heart that man believes, and it is therefore, with his heart, that man determines his eternal destiny. Paul is saying that to be saved, a person must place his absolute trust in the finished work of Christ (Proverbs 3:5–6).

True belief in the Lordship of Jesus Christ and in his resurrection comes from the heart. Your heart brings justification! *Believe in your heart.* Belief is the inward sign of the grace of Christ working in your life (Luke 6:45). Justification is a legal term that indicates a person has been made right with the accuser. Literally, Christ gave himself so we could be right with God.

True Christianity is far more than just head knowledge of Jesus. Many people who think they are saved are not, because they have never received Jesus into their hearts by faith. They believe in their heads but not in their hearts. They are missing heaven by eighteen inches, the distance from one's heart to one's brain.

Paul wants the lost to know that anything less than total trust in the Lord Jesus will not produce salvation but will lead the sinner straight to Hell. Too many people are trying to hold Jesus with one hand and other things with the other (Jesus plus church; Jesus plus baptism; etc.). This will not work! Salvation is Jesus plus nothing! That is made clear in the Word of God.

The promises. When we come to faith in Jesus Christ the right way—God's way—we are then given some precious promises. Notice what they are.

- *Assurance in Romans 10:11.* We are reminded here that when we trust Jesus according to God's plan, we will never be disappointed. We will never hear him tell us, "I'm sorry, but I can't save you." Instead, we will hear him say, "Well done thou good and faithful servant." No one who trusts Jesus for their soul's salvation need to ever fear losing it!
- *Acceptance in Romans 10:12.* This verse tells us that God does not play favorites. Anyone who hears his call and responds in faith will be saved by the grace of God. When we come to the Lord by faith, we will be saved and accepted of him.

- *Amnesty in Romans 10:13.* Here, the promise is confirmed. We are reminded that whosoever calls on the name of the Lord will be saved. To "call upon the Lord" meant to seek God in the way he had prescribed. So when someone says, "God and I have an arrangement," you know that they are lost. They may be calling on the lord, but they are not calling on the Lord Jesus! No one who comes will be turned away (John 6:37). When God saves a soul, he saves that soul forever (Ephesians 4:30).

The evangelistic appeal

The definition of evangelism: Effectively engaging unbelievers with a witness and testimony that will draw them to Christ is one of our primary purposes for living. Reaching others for Jesus Christ is one of our main purposes in life as a Christian,

Every believer is commissioned to bring people to Jesus. Can one be faithful in evangelism without giving an appeal? The basis of our evangelistic appeal must be eternal life found in Christ Jesus, and that if anyone would find this life, he or she must accept Jesus as his Lord and personal Savior. The message must be clear and plain. It must be clear to the hearers what it is you wish them to do. When making an appeal, our goal is not to win an argument but to win souls. The goal is to see unbelievers fall in love with Jesus.

The folk of our witness is Jesus Christ. Paul defined the gospel as the death, burial, and resurrection of Jesus Chris. If we aren't explaining the sacrifice of Christ, then we're not really sharing the gospel. An important part of this theme is the fact that Jesus Christ is the only way to salvation, not just one of many ways. "I am the way, the truth and the life. No one comes to the Father except through me" (John 14:6). The power of our witness is the Holy Spirit. It is the Spirit who transforms a life, and a transformed life is evident to all. As we witness, we must spend much time in prayer, allowing the Spirit's power to enable us to let our light shine in a way that others will recognize the power of God in us. We must be familiar enough with the Scriptures to accurately present the Gospel to others. "Always be prepared to give an answer to everyone who asks you to give the reason for the hope that you have" (1 Peter 3:15).

Use a testimonial approach in appealing to unbelievers; this often works. Instead of placing the people on the spot by asking them questions about themselves, share your story with them. This means that you communicate the Gospel to them by using yourself as an example. In your testimony, tell how you answered God's call on your heart to repent and believe the gospel and how God saved you by his grace, through faith in Jesus Christ.

The Holy Spirit knows the hearts of men and women better than we do, therefore, we must trust his leading more than our own when evangelizing others. We must be willing to be led by the Spirit in both word and circumstance, because evangelism cannot simply happen on our own terms. In Acts 8:26–40, the desert was an unlikely location for evangelism, but Philip saw it as a divine appointment.

Paul spoke of this truth in 1 Corinthians 3:6, he wrote, "I planted, Apollos watered, but God gave the growth." When we share the gospel with unbelievers, we must rely upon the sovereignty of God to bring about the new birth. It's not the clichés of man, nor is it the power of the presentation. The power is in God's message and the new birth comes as the wind blows, and we can't control the wind. We see the evidence of it, but we can't control it.

John Piper, the Chancellor of Bethlehem College and Seminary gave this analogy of a sailboat. He said (when reading the manual on how to use a sailboat) it says on the front of the manual: "All you need to know for successful sailing." So the manual claims to be a sufficient guide for sailing. On page 6 of the manual you read, "Before hoisting the sail, be sure that you know the way the wind is blowing so as to put the rigging in proper position to avoid capsizing or injury." So you go out on the lake with the boat, and before you hoist the sail, you hold a little cloth in the air to see which way the wind is blowing.

Suppose somebody said, "Hey, why are you lifting that cloth in the air to find out which way the wind is blowing? The manual says that it contains everything you need to know for successful sailing.

Shouldn't you just look in the manual to learn which way the wind is blowing?"

That's the kind of mistake many people make, I think, when they say that we should not be like Philip today and listen for the special direction of the Spirit in personal evangelism. The Bible doesn't rule out that special guidance, and the Bible doesn't take its place.

We witness because we love Christ. We witness because he loves us. We witness because we want to honor and obey him. We witness because he gives us a special love for others.

God wants you to witness because of the benefits he offers to those who receive Christ: They become children of God, their bodies become temples of God, and all of their sins are forgiven. They begin to experience the peace and love of God, and they receive God's direction and purpose for their lives. They experience the power of God to change their lives, and they have the assurance of eternal life.

The assurance of salvation

To be an effective disciple, it is imperative that we not only be saved, but that we also be sure of our salvation. God does not want us to be in doubt about the most important thing in life and eternity. For a disciple of Jesus Christ, assurance is not only possible, but it is necessary. Without assurance, there can be no real peace or joy in the Christian life. We must have the assurance of our salvation if we are going to grow strong and effective disciples of Jesus Christ.

If you are born again, you can never be unborn. In John 3:3–4, Nicodemus wasn't too sure about his salvation, in fact, he really couldn't understand salvation at all. So he came to Jesus by night and heard the Lord say to him, "You must be born again." Nicodemus; was puzzled. He wanted to know from Jesus, "Can a man enter his mother's womb and be born again?" No, he can't, because once you are born physically, you can't be "unborn" physically. The same is true in the spiritual realm; once you are born spiritually, you can't be "unborn" spiritually. The new birth can't be reversed; no more than a newborn baby can somehow crawl back into the womb of its mother.

It can't be done. If you are born again, it is forever, and you can never be "unborn."

God did not save us to lose us as we make our way home to heaven. He saved us by his grace, and he saved us for all eternity. It was not our works that saved us, and it is not our works that keep us! We are saved by grace (Ephesians 2:8); and we are kept by grace, and we are secured by grace.

Assurance is found the Word *of God.* The word of God is the written record of God's plans and desire for us. It speaks with God's authority about our salvation. It confirms, in writing, the assurance of our salvation. We can be saved and know it beyond any shadow of doubt because of the Word of God.

The apostle John wrote in 1 John 5:13, "These things have I written unto you, that believe on the name of the Son of God, that ye may know that ye have eternal life and that ye may believe on the name of the son of God." John says that you can know for certain that you have eternal life.

We have a written contract assuring us of our eternal salvation in the Word of God (1 John 5:13) Once God gives salvation to a person, no one can snatch us out of the eternal protection of his almighty hand (John 10:28, 29).

God wants you to have the confident assurance that if you were to die today, that you would have no doubt that you'd go to heaven. We know we have eternal life because of the promises in God's Word. He promises eternal life to all who trust in Jesus Christ as Lord and Savior.

We must draw our assurance from faith in the facts of the Word of God and not from our feelings. Our faith and our assurance must stand on the promises of the Word of God rather than on our feelings.

Philippians 1:6 says, "Being confident of this very thing, that he which hath begun a good work in you will perform it until the day of Jesus Christ." The word "confidence" means "fully persuaded, to be convinced beyond all doubt." Paul is telling us we can have absolute assurance that if you have accepted Jesus Christ as Lord and Savior, you are saved, and that you will go to Heaven! Paul had reached the conclusion that, "What God starts he will finish." He was simply saying, "I have no doubt about the outcome."

Assurance is found in the work *of Christ.* Just as our salvation comes from believing in Jesus Christ alone, so does our assurance. "Neither is there salvation in any other, for there is no other name under heaven given among men, whereby we must be saved" (Acts 4:12). Only Jesus Christ, being God in human form, could die in order to save sinners from the guilt and power of sin. When we receive Jesus Christ, he removes our guilt and we receive forgiveness for our sins. We immediately begin a new life with his resurrection power, and we have a future assurance that we will spend eternity in heaven with him.

If you want to have assurance of your salvation, it is necessary to believe that Christ will never leave you, abandon you, or disown you as his child. When you trust Jesus Christ as your Savior for the forgiveness of your sins, you will also find the assurance of salvation. John 1:12 says, "But as many as received him, to them gave he power to become the sons of God even to them that who believe on his name." Once you become a child of God, the Lord will never disown but will receive you as one of His own.

The name Jesus means "Yahweh saves," and Jesus, the Son of God, became incarnate to save us from sin and death. The Bible tells us Jesus came to save sinners (1 Timothy 1:15) and to seek and save the lost (Luke 19:10); and that whoever believes in Jesus will be saved (John 3:16).

Assurance is found in the witness *of the Holy Spirit.* Understanding the witness of the Holy Spirit in the life of a disciple is very important. The Holy Spirit verifies that we are children of God. The presence of the Spirit within us provides us with the assurance that God dwells in us, and we dwell in him.

To understand and believe in the Gospel requires a supernatural work of God's Spirit in your heart. Romans 8:16 teaches that the assurance of salvation is part of the ministry of the Holy Spirit. "The Spirit himself bears witness with our spirit that we are children of God." The things which the Spirit of God witnesses to us gives us the assurance that we are (sons) children of God.

The witness of the Spirit is not for the satisfaction of others, but it is for satisfaction of the children of God themselves, who may be ready to doubt at times.

The Spirit, when he comes inside you, witnesses to that fact that Jesus knows you. He helps you know and to understand that Jesus died for you on Calvary, and that God has forgiven you of your sins and has received you into his own family. He also gives you a desire to be with God and to pray to him and to read his Word. Then the Spirit of God makes your spirit new inside of you so that your own spirit rejoices to obey God and wants to obey him.

The Holy Spirit's witness does not occur continually. But it happens as we pray. His witness occurs within us when our human spirits cry out to God saying, "Abba Father" (Romans 8:15)—his witness to God the Father, not to us. God the Father rejoices and delights in being reminded, by the Holy Spirit and by you that we are his children.

Abba is the Aramaic word for Father; in the English language it is like "Daddy" or "Papa." Jesus used this word for God in the Garden of Gethsemane when He called out, "Abba Father." These words help us to remember that we are God's children by grace and point us to our Savior and salvation. They also help us be assured of our intimate relationship with God the Father because of Jesus Christ. For we don't call God, "Sir," "Master," "buddy," or "friend," but "Father."

Paul says, "The Spirit himself beareth witness with our spirit that we are children of God, and if children, then heirs; heirs of God, and joint-heirs with Christ, if so be that we suffer with him, that we may be also glorified together" (Romans 8:16–17). We are heirs of God and co-heirs with Jesus Christ. We inherit eternal life, the new Heaven, the new earth, and all that is his. We are recipients of his promises—his promises of mercy, grace, and love. As God's children, we will face hardships because of this identity. But we can be comforted that these things lead to glory.

Bibliography

Bonhoeffer, Dietrich, *The Cost of Discipleship* (New York: Macmillan, 1966).

Bugbee, Bruce, *What You Do Best in the Body of Christ* (Grand Rapids, Michigan: Zondervan, 1995).

Christopherson, Jeff, *Kingdom First* (Nashville, Tennessee: B&H Publishing Group, 2015).

Evans, Tony, *Our God Is Awesome* (Chicago, Renaissance Productions: Moody Press, 1994).

Law, Terry, *The Power of Praise and Worship* (Tulsa, OK: Victory House Publishers, 1985).

MacDonald, James, *Gripped by the Greatness of God* (Chicago: Moody Publishers, 2005).

Ogden, Greg, *Discipleship Essentials*, Expanded Edition (Downer Grove, Ill.: Intervarsity Press, 2007).

Piper, John, *Desiring God* (Portland, Oregon: Multnomah Press, 1986).

Powell, Paul W., *Dynamic Discipleship* (Nashville, Tennessee: Broadman Press, 1984).

Sorge, Bob, *Exploring Worship: A Practical Guide to Praise and Worship* (New York: Oasis House, 1987).

Warren, Rick, *The Purpose Driven Life* (Grand Rapids, Michigan: Zondervan, 2002).

———, *What's driving your church?* (Pastors.com community, 2017).

Whitney, Donald S., *Spiritual Disciplines for the Christian Life* (Colorado Springs, CO: NavPress, 1991).

Wiersbe, Warren W., *Real Worship* (Nashville, TN: Oliver Nelson, 1986), 27.

Wilkes, C. Gene, *Jesus on Leadership* (Nashville, Tenn.: Lifeway Press, 1996).

About the Author

Bishop Joel Nelson is the founder and president of Making Disciples Ministry. He began his ministry in 1980, helping to plant churches in Prince Georges County, Maryland. He planted and pastored New Jericho Baptist Church in Laurel, Maryland, in 1982. In 1999, Joel became a part of the staff at the Fredericksburg Area Baptist Network, serving more than fifty churches in the Fredericksburg area. During his tenure of serving as director of church development, he helped to strengthen many of the churches that were declining and helped to plant several new churches. His work with the Fredericksburg Area Baptist Network allowed him the opportunity to lead several mission teams to various places around the world such as South Africa, Italy, Jamaica, and the Bahamas. He has also served on mission teams in Austria, Rome, and in parts of the New England area.

Prior to his current role, he planted New Destiny Baptist Church in Fredericksburg, Virginia, where he served as pastor for seven years. The church placed a special emphasis on making disciples, with a vision and theme of "Making Disciples That Make a Difference."

Joel and his wife Ethel resides in Fredericksburg, Virginia, and are blessed with one son, Kevin. Through his headquarters in Fredericksburg, Virginia, he coordinates his ministry and ministers in the areas of discipleship and mission throughout the United States and other countries.

CPSIA information can be obtained
at www.ICGtesting.com
Printed in the USA
BVHW081507050819
555095BV00007B/927/P